How God Supplies Your Every Need

by
Jerry Savelle

HOW GOD SUPPLIES YOUR EVERY NEED
Formerly *Living To Give*

ISBN 1-888152-02-8

Unless otherwise stated, all Scripture
quotations are taken from the
King James Version of the Bible.

Jerry Savelle Ministries International
P.O. Box 748
Crowley, Texas 76036
(817) 297-3155

Contents

Introduction 7

1 Stop Being Need-Minded 11

2 Why God Wants Your Needs Met 39

3 Giving Produces Receiving 63

4 Giving As A Lifestyle 85

5 Why Your Giving Is Important
To God 107

References 125

Introduction

Recently, I was invited to take part in a week-long believers' convention. The first time I came to the platform to speak, I had to admit to the audience:

"I have no idea what I'm going to be ministering during the course of these meetings. I only know what I'm going to speak about today. But, in praying about this convention, I was told by the Lord:

'I want you to go prepared, prayed up, sensitive to the Holy Ghost. Don't try to prearrange study notes or make detailed outlines. Just be available to speak what I am going to lay on your heart.'

"Then the Lord spoke something in my spirit which I am to share with you this first day. He said, 'I want you to speak with a prophetic utterance. I want you to prepare My people for what is to come in the days ahead.'"

What I spoke to those faithful believers in that series of meetings is the basic message which I have condensed into book form to share with you in these pages. I pray that it will speak to you as it did to those who heard it as I brought it forth under the direction and inspiration of the Holy Spirit. I am convinced that it is a message of God for these days on the vital subject of giving.

In my talks I was led of the Spirit, step by step, day by day, to deliver the important message the Lord was revealing to my heart. The Apostle Paul once wrote to the Roman Christians, telling them, *I desire to come to you that I might impart to you a spiritual gift* (Romans1:11). That's the way I went to that meeting, with the God-motivated intention of sharing a spiritual gift with those who would be willing to open their hearts and minds to hear what the Spirit is saying to the church in these crucial times. That same Spirit-instilled message is the one which I will be sharing with you in these few chapters.

It is my sincere prayer that God will be magnified in what you read. I also pray that you and every other person who reads this book will see Jesus on every page. I ask the heavenly Father to anoint me as I deliver this message, and to anoint you as you receive it. I thank the Lord that He has given us access to the deep things of God, the ability to understand mysteries. I praise Him that He has filled us with the very Revealer of all mysteries, the Holy Spirit Himself. Finally, I pray that you will draw from this book the revelation, instruction, inspiration and direction - the spiritual gift - that the Holy Spirit wants to impart to you so you will be blessed and in turn become a blessing to many others. Like Paul, I thank the Lord upon every remembrance of you, and I pray that God's richest blessing will be yours in abundance.

1

Stop Being
Need-Minded

1

STOP BEING NEED-MINDED

Some time ago I was scheduled to fly to Tulsa, Oklahoma, to speak in a meeting. Before I left home, I tried to talk to the Lord about some critical needs in my life and ministry. Instead of answering the way I had expected, He told me, "When you get to Tulsa, I want you to give away your van." I dropped the subject.

On the plane, I again approached the Lord about my pressing situation: "Father, I really need to talk to You about my needs," I told Him, "It just seems they have become overwhelming."

Again the Lord spoke to me and said, "When you get to Tulsa, I want you to give away your van." So again I dropped the subject.

A while later, I got into a conversation with Meadowlark Lemon who was traveling with me. We were looking at some sports articles in <u>USA Today</u> and discussing them. Then, in a quiet moment, I once more took up my "case" with the Lord: "Father, during this meeting in Tulsa, I am going to have a little time between services, and I really need to talk to You about my needs."

Once more there came His response, "When you get to Tulsa, I want you to give away your van." But this time He went on: "Also, there are five preachers in Tulsa who have become discouraged and are about to give up the ministry. I want you to give each of them a suit of clothes." So once more I decided not to continue the discussion.

Finally, I just couldn't hold back any longer. I said to the Lord: "Father, I've just got to talk to You! You know we've been building our international headquarters in Fort Worth this year. We have moved into them, but there are still lots of things we need. More land, for instance, and more buildings. But we just don't have the money to get what we need..."

"When you get to Tulsa, I want you to give away your van and five suits of clothes." It was then that it finally hit me what was happening. Every time I tried to talk to God about my need, He talked to me about seed.

Now that's not deep. As children of God, all of us should understand it. We are seed-planting people. But, if you are like me, you have probably noticed that over the past couple of years your needs have grown larger and larger. You must be wondering, as I was on that plane, *where in the world is the money going to come from to meet my steadily increasing obligations?*

I believe the Lord showed me the answer to that important question while I was in that airplane on my way to Tulsa. What He revealed to me is what I am sharing with you now in this book. After telling me several times to give, when all I wanted to talk about was receiving, the Lord told me: "In the days to come, the needs of the Body of Christ are going to become so great that, in the natural, they will appear to be impossible to meet. But I am telling you now: don't wait until then to get busy sowing seed into the Kingdom, because your needs are already enormous. Don't wait until you get an answer to your present needs before you begin to prepare for your future needs."

Then He made a statement that suddenly put the whole subject into perspective for me:

"You must become seed-conscious, not need-conscious."

Becoming Seed-Minded

If you and I are going to successfully deal with the issues of life on God's level, then we are going to have to get His viewpoint and perspective. We are going to have to learn to operate the way God operates. We must learn to think and act the way our heavenly Father thinks and acts. That's why He showed me that every time I tried to talk to Him about answering my need, He spoke to me about planting seed: the Lord will only discuss solutions, not problems.

Our Father is well aware that the needs of the Body of Christ are growing at a tremendous rate every year. He realizes that the entire Church is consumed with needs. I know that, personally, I have never had so many needs in my whole life as I have been experiencing the past year or so. I'm working harder now than I ever have before. It almost seems that the harder I work, the more needs I produce. Every time my faith grows, my need grows right along with it.

The same is true of you: every time your faith reaches a new, higher dimension, so does the need that faith venture produces. What it took to keep you going last year is not nearly enough to keep you afloat this year. Why? Because your needs increase as your faith, your ministry and your sphere of influence grows and expands. That's natural. The danger in all of this otherwise healthy growth and expansion is that if we are not careful, we will become need-oriented.

That's what I believe the Devil is trying to do to the Body of Christ today: make us need-conscious. He doesn't so much place new needs upon us; they come as a natural result of our growth, expansion and outreach. The deeper we penetrate into enemy territory, the more resistance we meet from our enemy and the greater our need for larger and larger amounts of supplies. So our adversary, the Devil, seeing he can't stop our advance, sets in to cause us problems. He begins throwing up obstacles in our paths, setting "booby traps," laying ambushes, sniping away at us from all sides - doing his best to disrupt our vital supply lines.

In short, Satan is going all out to pressure us into taking our minds off our objectives and goals, and focusing them on our problems.

In our Christian battle, you and I must not become need-oriented. If we do, we will give into pressure and become discouraged. If we keep our attention and our eyes trained on our seemingly impossible needs, we will be tempted to give up the fight and quit. That's exactly what the enemy wants us to do.

Our Needs Are Already Provided For

There is a way out of this situation: His name is Jesus. Our Lord had needs when He walked this earth giving His life in ministry to others. One time He was preparing to enter Jerusalem, you remember the story, how He sent two of His disciples ahead into the city. He told them that in a certain place they would find a young colt, which no man had ever ridden. They were to untie the colt and bring it back to Him. If anybody asked what they were doing taking the animal, they were to answer, *...the Lord hath need of him...* (Mark 11:3).

So we see from this statement that Jesus did have needs. But was His mind centered on His needs? Does God in heaven spend His time pondering and worrying over the needs of His children, His Church, or the world?

What has the Lord said to us about our needs? Has He just told us to "grin and bear it" until we "all get to heaven" where we won't have any more needs? Or, has He indicated that there is an answer to our needs, here and now?

I remember when Brother Kenneth Copeland first came to my home town and began preaching the message which was to revolutionize my life. It was brand new to me then. I had never heard anything like it. But I believed it, and I wanted to know more about it.

Some time later, I was talking with Brother Copeland and I told him: "I believe your message, and I'm doing all

I know to do to put it into practice in my life. I understand how some things work in the Kingdom of God. I understand how healing comes, and all of that. But there is one thing I don't understand: I just don't know how you talk God into meeting your needs."

I will never forget what Brother Copeland told me that day. He said: "Jerry, God has already done all He is going to do about your needs."

"You're kidding!" I answered. "He's not going to leave me in this mess, is He?"

That was not what Brother Copeland meant. He wasn't saying that God was not going to do anything about my situation. What he meant was that God had already done everything necessary to meet my every need.

Jesus does not have to hang on the cross and die, over and over again, every time somebody needs to be saved. God has already met the need for salvation of all mankind, forever. He is just waiting for each individual person to receive by faith what He has already provided by grace.

The same is true of all our physical and material needs. God has already made provision for our salvation from poverty, lack and want, just as He has already made provision for our salvation from sin and death. This provision was paid for by the death, burial, resurrection and ascension of our Lord and Savior, Jesus Christ, Who now sits at the right hand of the throne of God where ...*he ever liveth to make intercession for (us)*... (Hebrews. 7:25) But the actual terms of this provision were spelled out long ago in the Old Testament.

The Blessings of the Covenant

And it shall come to pass, if thou shalt hearken diligently unto the voice of the Lord thy God, to observe and to do all his commandments which I command thee this day, that the Lord thy God will set thee on high above all nations of the earth:

And all these blessings shall come on thee, and overtake thee, if thou shalt hearken unto the voice of the Lord thy God.

Blessed shalt thou be in the city, and blessed shalt thou be in the field.

Blessed shall be the fruit of thy body, and the fruit of thy ground, and the fruit of thy cattle, the increase of thy kine, and the flocks of thy sheep.

Blessed shall be thy basket and thy store.

Blessed shalt thou be when thou comest in, and blessed shalt thou be when thou goest out.

The Lord shall cause thine enemies that rise up against thee to be smitten before thy face: they shall come out against thee one way, and flee before thee seven ways.

The Lord shall command the blessing upon thee in thy storehouses, and in all that thou settest thine hand unto; and he shall bless thee in the land which the Lord thy God giveth thee.

The Lord shall establish thee an holy people unto himself, as he hath sworn unto thee, if thou shalt keep the commandments of the Lord thy God, and walk in his ways.

And all people of the earth shall see that thou art called by the name of the Lord, and they shall be afraid of thee. And the Lord shall make thee plenteous in goods, in the fruit of thy body, and in the fruit of thy cattle, and in the fruit of thy ground, in the land which the Lord sware unto thy fathers to give thee.

The Lord shall open unto thee his good treasure, the heaven to give the rain unto thy land in his season, and to bless all the work of thine hand: and thou shalt lend unto many nations, and thou shalt not borrow.

. And the Lord shall make thee the head, and not the tail; and thou shalt be above only, and thou shalt not be beneath; if that thou hearken unto the commandments of the Lord thy God, which I command thee this day, to observe and to do them;

And thou shalt not go aside from any of the words which I command thee this day, to the right hand, or to the left, to go after other gods to serve them.

Deuteronomy 28:1-14

Notice verse 11:   *The Lord will make thee plenteous in goods...* Let's read it in *The New International Version*: *The Lord will grant you abundant prosperity...*

Now, according to the Covenant, what does God think about our needs? Obviously He is deeply interested in us and our circumstances of life. If fact, He is so deeply concerned that He has made provision for all of our earthly needs. He told the children of Israel that if they would listen to His Word and walk in faithful obedience to Him, He would see to it that all kinds of blessings would come upon them and overtake them. One of those blessings was that they would be made "plenteous in goods."

Well, what happens to your needs if you are made "plenteous in goods," if you have "abundant prosperity?" Your needs are met. Not only are your needs met, you have enough left over to help others in need.

The Living Bible translates verse 11: *The Lord will give you an abundance of good things... The Revised Standard Version* says: *...the Lord will make you abound in prosperity...*

In this passage the Lord is telling us that if we obey Him, we will be so blessed that we won't have to borrow from others; instead, we will lend to many. In verse 13 He has promised us that if we are obedient to Him, we will be *the head, and not the tail, ...above only, ...and not.... beneath. The Living Bible* says, *...you shall always have the upper hand.* I like that.

Now those are the blessings of the Covenant which God made with His people, the descendants of Abraham. Do you recall what the Apostle Paul said about us Christians? *And if ye be Christ's, then are ye Abraham's seed, and heirs according to the promise* (Galatians 3:29). What promise is he talking about here? The promise that God will meet our every need - spiritual, physical and material.

We sing about our wonderful Covenant with the Lord. We joyfully proclaim and confess that the blessings of Abraham are ours. Well, if that is true, then we have every right to expect God to make us "plenteous in goods." I am not the one who made that promise, nor was it Paul, or even Moses; it was God Himself.

God has promised to make you and me "plenteous in goods." But that does not mean that we are to seek after "all these things." We're not. We are to ...*seek first the kingdom of God, and his righteousness*... (Matthew 6:33). We are not to "pursue" prosperity; but then we don't have to. The Covenant promises us that if we hearken diligently unto the Lord our God and faithfully serve Him, all these blessings will "pursue" us; they will come upon us and overtake us.

No, I'm not seeking or pursuing goods or abundance or prosperity. My eyes are on the Creator, not the creation. I am seeking first the Kingdom of God and His righteousness, knowing that as I do, all these things I need will be added to me as well.

Many critics of this message say that we preach and practice the pursuit of prosperity, a seeking after "things." If that were so, it would be a terrible indictment. But it's not so. We are not pursuing goods, nor are we teaching others to pursue them. What we are preaching and practicing is the pursuit of God. But we also know and testify to the fact that the Lord has promised that as we seek Him and His righteousness, He will give us an abounding prosperity. We expect the Lord to keep His Word. We expect to be blessed, to be made prosperous, to have all of our needs met, *to have the upper hand*, as *The Living Bible* says.

I want that kind of life. What about you? I'm tired of being the tail; I want to be the head. I'm tired of being on the bottom; I want to be on the top. I'm tired of being the underdog; I want to have the upper hand. And all of that is part of the Covenant between my God and me.

So, we know what God thinks of our needs. He has seen them and has made abundant provision for them. He has promised in His Word to see to it that we have plenty for our own needs and enough left over to meet the needs of others.

According to the Covenant, abundance is our heritage as the seed of Abraham. His blessing is our blessing. And what blessing did God pronounce upon Abraham?

And I will make of thee a great nation, and I will bless thee, and make thy name great; and thou shalt be a blessing.
And I will bless them that bless thee, and curse him that curseth thee: and in thee shall all families of the earth be blessed.

Genesis 12:2,3

This is the heritage of the saints: to be blessed, and to be a blessing to all families (nations) of the earth.

The Curse of the Law

But it shall come to pass, if thou wilt not hearken unto the voice of the Lord thy God, to observe to do all his commandments and his statutes which I command thee this day; that all these curses shall come upon thee, and overtake thee.

Deuteronomy 28:15

Notice that this verse states what will happen if you and I are not obedient to the Lord. The Covenant includes a curse as well as a blessing. To the faithful and obedient, God promises blessings beyond measure, but to the unfaithful and disobedient He promises even more abundant curses. In verses 15 to 68 (a section several times longer than the section of blessing!) each of these curses - including poverty, lack and want - is spelled out in full detail:

Because thou servedst not the Lord thy God with joyfulness, and with gladness of heart, for the abundance of all things;

Therefore shalt thou serve thine enemies which the Lord shall send against thee, in hunger, and in thirst, and in nakedness, and in want of all things....

Deuteronomy 28:47,48

From these passages it seems clear that if a person is not having his needs met by the Lord, then he must be serving his enemies - he must be operating under the curse of the law.

If your needs are never fully met, if you are continually struggling with the same basic needs all the time, there is every reason to conclude that you are operating under the curse rather than under the blessings of God's Covenant with His people.

Now notice that I did not say that having needs is a curse. That is not true, because we all have needs; I have as many as you do, maybe more. I said that having continually unfulfilled needs is a strong indication of operating under the curse.

The New Testament clearly declares that as Christians you and I have been redeemed from the curse: *Christ hath redeemed us from the curse of the law, being made a curse for us...* (Galatians 3:13). Jesus said He did not come to abolish the Law or the prophets, but to fulfill them (Matthew 5:17). We qualify for the blessing of the Covenant, not the curse. The blessing of the Covenant includes the meeting of all our needs. Therefore, if we have constant, unfulfilled needs, then it logically follows that something must be wrong.

That's why I say that as believers, it is a curse not to have our needs met.

God's Knowledge of Our Needs

"But that is the Old Covenant," you say. "What about the New Covenant?" In the New Testament, Jesus told us, *...your Father knoweth what things ye have need of, before ye ask him* (Matthew 6:8). Later on, God spoke through the Apostle Paul, assuring us that He will supply all our need according to His riches in glory by Christ Jesus (Philippians 4:19).

So when we go before the Lord about our needs, we are not springing on Him something He is not aware of. He already knows what our needs are before we ask. What the Lord showed me in all this is the fact that when we spend hours and hours in prayer, day after day, going into great detail about our every need, we are wasting His time and ours.

Well, if that is not the way we are to go to the Lord about our needs, how should we approach Him? Hebrews 4:16 gives us the answer: *Let us therefore come boldly unto the throne of grace, that we may obtain mercy, and find grace to help in time of need.*

What is God telling us? He is saying: "Dearly beloved, I know all about your needs before you come to Me. I have promised to supply all your need according to My riches in glory by Christ Jesus. Don't fret, don't worry or strain; just come to Me and freely receive all that I have given you in Christ."

So we see God's attitude about our needs. He is not need-oriented, and He doesn't want us to be. To come before Him and spend hours discussing our needs is to put the emphasis on the wrong thing. It is also insulting to the Lord, because we are acting as though He is unwilling to meet our needs as He has promised, or that He is not aware, that we have to "inform" Him of what is going on and what needs to be done about it.

God's Provision for Meeting Needs

What about supplying those needs? It is fine to say that

God knows what we need before we ask, and that He is willing to provide what we need according to His riches in glory by Christ Jesus, but how do we get Him to do what He says He is willing to do?

Think about this for a moment: if we are not to waste God's time nor ours talking about our needs, what are we to talk to the Lord about? I believe you know the answer already. The Lord is saying, "Now that we've got your needs out of the way, let's talk about seeds." Now that is a subject that our heavenly Father will discuss all day long.

You see, God is not need-oriented, He is seed-oriented. I kept telling God about my need and He kept talking to me about my seed. I wanted to focus on what I did not have, God wanted to focus on what I did have. That's the way God always works.

In Ephesians 4:28 Paul writes: *Let him that stole steal no more: but rather let him labor, working with his hands the thing which is good, that he may have to give to him that needeth.* So here is the primary reason you and I are to work - so that we will have seed to sow.

When most people want to know what your profession is, they will ask, "What do you do for a living?" God doesn't consider your labor something you do for a living. God says that we don't work for a living, we work for a giving.

Can you imagine being blessed so abundantly, being so prosperous, so plenteous in goods, that your entire wage or salary was seed to be invested in the lives of others?

The point I am making is that God is not need-conscious; He is seed-conscious. When God had "needs" of His own, He fulfilled those needs by giving. He "needed" the redemption of mankind; He "needed" a family. So what did He do? He planted a seed; He gave Jesus.

Our Lord told us plainly, ...*Except a corn of wheat fall into the ground and die, it abideth alone: but if it die, it bringeth forth much fruit* (John 12:24). God sowed His "Seed," His only Son Jesus, into the earth, and reaped in return a harvest of sons and daughters. He planted the best seed heaven had to offer, not worthless seed. He didn't look for some old, decrepit, worn-out angel to use as seed, someone who was no longer needed. No, He chose and planted the very best He had. And He reaped the best of all harvests, human souls. The Lord got that family He wanted - us!

God is seed-conscious. So He's not going to talk to us very long about our needs, as real and vital as they may be. After all, He knows all about them before we ask. Instead He has made provision for the meeting of every last one of our needs. He invites us to come boldly to His throne of grace to obtain mercy and to find grace in our time of need. As we do, He will talk to us about seed.

Leadership Giving

Now I want to tell you what God in His grace did for the churches in Macedonia.

Though they have been going through much trouble and hard

times, they have mixed their wonderful joy with their deep poverty, and the result has been an overflow of giving to others.

2 Corinthians 8:2 (TLB)

It is time for us to become leaders in the spirit of cheerful giving. If there is any one thing which has impressed me about Kenneth and Gloria Copeland during the twenty-five years I have worked with them, it is their leadership in giving. It is the reason they are so blessed. Many people don't see what goes on in the background of their ministry, behind the scenes of their personal lives. I don't see it all, of course, but I do probably see more than most people. And I can testify that the Copelands are wonderful examples of leaders in the spirit of cheerful giving.

Now that is a virtue I have had to learn gradually over a long period of time. When I first started out in the ministry, I was not blessed with the understanding of this principle.

I will never forget the first time Brother Copeland asked me to come to his room and pray with him. That was way back in 1972. After two or three days of meeting for times of intense prayer, Brother Copeland announced, "The Lord has told me that in order for us to launch into this television ministry, I am to give away my airplane."

Now since I remembered that we had flown to that meeting in that very plane, my first question was: "How are we going to get home?"

Now that was real "seed-consciousness" on my part. You can see what level I was operating on. All I could think about was our need. But I soon learned better, and so can you.

The point is that Brother Copeland was "seed-conscious" and I wasn't. I was "need-conscious."

But then Brother Copeland went a step further. He announced that since the engines had a lot of flight time on them, he was going to have them repaired before he gave the airplane away.

I thought to myself, "That's crazy, let the man you give it to do that." For the life of me I couldn't figure why anyone would spend several thousand dollars to repair a plane he was about to give away. Then I discovered the reasoning behind that action.

Brother Copeland explained, "The reason I want to put this plane in first-class condition is because by giving it away I am planting a seed, and I don't want to reap a worn-out plane in return."

Now when most of us are called upon to give away some of our possessions, such as clothing, we usually go through our closets and pick out everything we don't like: whatever is worn, out of style, misfitting, uncomfortable, unbecoming or just plain ugly. What a sacrifice! If you do that, do you know what you are going to get in return for each old cast-off garment you give? An abundant return of exactly the same thing!

If you and I are to be leaders in giving, we must give the way God gives; we must give the best. Then the best will come back to us, in multiplied form. That is a lesson I learned from the Copelands. I saw their example and the results it produced, and I decided to follow that example.

I am not giving you an order; I am not saying you must do it, but others are eager for it. This is one way to prove that your love is real, that it goes beyond mere words.

2 Corinthians 8:8 (TLB)

In the hard times in which you and I are now living, people need a good example. In these days when there are so many ministries failing, so many churches cutting back or shutting down, so many believers becoming discouraged, being sidetracked and dropping out, there are multitudes begging for someone to stand up and provide them an example and a model. That example and model should be us, the saints of God who are the leaders in cheerful giving.

Finish What You Started

You know how full of love and kindness our Lord Jesus was: though he was so very rich yet to help you he became so very poor, so that by being poor he could make you rich. I want to suggest that you finish what you started to do a year ago...

2 Corinthians 8:9,10 (TLB)

Now that speaks to many people in churches today. Many Christians began to live by the principles of God's Word, but then they came under pressure from the world, from Satan and from those who oppose this message. They were deceived into giving up on sowing and reaping. The deception is not in teaching people how to give; it is talking them out of giving.

I am not going to be mislead by anyone who claims that this Biblical principle does not work. I am going to keep on doing what I have been practicing for two decades. I am going to finish what I started twenty-five years ago.

I want to suggest to you that you also "finish what you started." You may have come into this revelation some time ago. Maybe you began to prosper and grow, only to become disillusioned and discouraged by the abuses you saw within the movement and the criticism you heard about it from without. You may have been tempted to give up and to decide that perhaps it is not God's will for you to prosper after all.

You may have allowed certain negative reports and personal experiences to turn you away from believing in and practicing God's abundance. You may have turned back toward the old belief that God's will for His children is poverty, lack and want.

If so, I believe it is time to re-evaluate your situation. Complete what you began so well. Finish what you started.

Having started the ball rolling so enthusiastically, you should carry this project through to completion just as gladly, giving what-

ever you can out of whatever you have. Let your enthusiastic idea at the start be equaled by your realistic action now.

2 Corinthians 8:11 (TLB)

Don't ever lose your enthusiasm for giving and planting seeds. The greatest joys you will ever experience in your life will come in seeing God bless you so you can bless someone else.

That's also the reason the Devil doesn't want you to prosper. Because if you don't, you can't be a blessing to anybody else. We must quit being "need-conscious" and become "seed-conscious."

Needs Are Really Opportunities To Prosper

Let me close this chapter with one final illustration from scripture:

And Elijah the Tishbite, who was of the inhabitants of Gilead, said unto Ahab, As the Lord God of Israel liveth, before whom I stand, there shall not be dew nor rain these years, but according to my word.

And the word of the Lord came unto him, saying, Get thee hence, and turn thee eastward, and hide thyself by the brook Cherith, that is before Jordan.

And it shall be, that thou shalt drink of the brook; and I have commanded the ravens to feed thee there.

And it came to pass after a while, that the brook dried up, because there had been no rain in the land.

And the word of the Lord came unto him, saying,

Arise, get thee to Zarephath, which belongeth to Zidon, and dwell there: behold, I have commanded a widow woman there to sustain thee.

1 Kings 17:1-4, 7-9

Notice what the Lord said to the prophet in both these instances: *...I have commanded... the ravens to feed thee... a widow woman there to sustain thee...* Past tense. The Lord had already made provision for Elijah before He sent him on his way. In the case of the widow, even before God commanded Elijah to go to Zarephath, He had already given the woman orders to meet his needs.

So he arose and went to Zarephath. And then he came to the gate of the city, behold, the widow woman was there gathering of sticks: and he called to her, and said, Fetch me, I pray thee, a little water in a vessel, that I may drink.

And as she was going to fetch it, he called to her, and said, Bring me, I pray thee, a morsel of bread in thine hand.

And she said, As the Lord thy God liveth, I have not a cake, but an handful of meal in a barrel, and a little oil in a cruse: and, behold, I am gathering two sticks, that I may go in and dress it for me and my son, that we may eat it, and die.

And Elijah said unto her, Fear not; go and do as thou hast said: but make me thereof a little cake first, and bring it unto me, and after make for thee and for thy son.

For thus saith the Lord God of Israel, The barrel of meal shall not waste, neither shall the cruse of oil fail, until the day that the Lord sendeth rain upon the earth.

1 Kings 17:10-14

So this woman had already been instructed to care for the prophet. When he arrived, he asked her to feed him. But she was not "seed-conscious." She was "need-conscious." She said to him: "Oh, but you don't understand, prophet. I only have a few provisions which my son and I are about to eat and then die."

That's what many people are saying today. But that is not what God says about our situation.

I once heard Mike Murdock, a dynamic minister and musician, make a potent statement which I think bears repeating. He said, "Every time God gives you an opportunity to give, He is also giving you an opportunity to increase your income."

In this case, the Lord was giving this woman an opportunity to give because He wanted her to have an opportunity to have her needs met. But because she was so need-conscious, she couldn't recognize the wonderful opportunity that was being offered to her.

Every one of us has needs. Great needs. Pressing needs. And the Lord has many opportunities for us to give so we can have those needs met. But if we are like this poor widow, if we are "need-conscious," we will not recognize those opportunities for what they really are, opportunities to reap an abundant harvest.

The prophet told that poor woman to feed him first, promising her that if she would do so, then her provisions of meal and oil would not run out until the day of famine was over. Was he telling the truth?

And she went and did according to the saying of Elijah: and she, and he, and her house, did eat many days.

And the barrel of meal wasted not, neither did the cruse of oil fail, according to the word of the Lord, which he spake by Elijah.

1 Kings 17:15,16

I believe God is giving us an opportunity right now to prepare ourselves for what lies ahead down the road. He is commanding us to keep planting seeds, assuring us that if we do, our resources will not fail during the hard times to come. He is telling us to become "seed-conscious" rather than "need-conscious."

Prayer of Commitment

If the Lord has spoken to your heart through the pages of this chapter, repeat this prayer of commitment to Him out loud, right now:

Father, I thank You that You know all about my needs before I ever bring them to You. I thank You that I don't have to waste Your time or mine discussing them, begging You to meet them. I will not spend all my time talking about, or worrying about my needs. Instead I will trust them to You, knowing that they are under Your control.

Lord, I commit myself and my resources unto You. I trust You to meet my every need as You have promised in Your Word. No longer will I be "need-conscious," but I will be "seed-conscious." I will remember that I am a seed-planter.

Because I am a seed of Abraham and an heir to Your Covenant, You have promised to prosper me, to bless me and to make me to be a blessing to others. You have promised that if I will give to Your work and Your workers, You will multiply my meal and oil so that I may live and not die, but rather abound so I may be able to give to every good work.

I thank You, Lord, that I serve a Covenant-giving, Covenant-keeping God. You have promised to supply my needs according to Your riches in glory by Christ Jesus. Therefore, I submit my needs to You by planting seeds into Your Kingdom. I look for You to return them to me in an abundant harvest, for the sake of Your Kingdom.

For all these precious promises and wonderful blessings I give You thanks and praise, in Jesus' name. Amen.

2

WHY GOD WANTS
YOUR NEEDS MET

2

WHY GOD WANTS YOUR NEEDS MET

Therefore, as ye abound in every thing, in faith, and utterance, and knowledge, and in all diligence, and in your love to us, see that ye abound in this grace also.

2 Corinthians 8:7

Note that in this passage Paul states that he would like for Christians to ...*abound in this grace*... (NIV). The grace he is speaking of here is the grace of giving. In *The Living Bible* version which we examined in Chapter 1, this expression is called ...*the spirit of cheerful giving.*

Remember that these early Christians were going through ...*much trouble and hard times*... (2 Corinthians 8:2, TLB). You and I should be able to relate to that situation. In fact, so should every Christian. If you are going through "much trouble and hard times," you are in good company. I have often said that Satan attacks Christians only two times: when they have done something wrong, and when they have done something right.

Many believers get all upset when things go wrong, especially when they are trying so hard to do right. They somehow have the mistaken idea that their "doing good" ought to insure them against things "going bad." It doesn't. It certainly didn't for Paul and the first-century Christians.

Sometimes you and I will have the most trouble not because we are doing wrong, but precisely because we are doing right. The "going" has not always been smooth in my life. The reason the first part of my life wasn't smooth going is because I was out of the will of God.

But even now that I am in the center of God's will, things are not always smooth or easy. But the Lord always supplies the power and grace and everything else we need to come through the trouble and hard times. That too is part of the heritage of the saints.

But remember that the result of the trouble and hard times which the Early Church was going through was *an overflow of giving to others.* That is an important principle for us to learn today.

In my own case, I realized a long time ago that the quickest way to get my own needs met is to get involved in meeting the needs of someone else.

The Purpose For God's Blessings

I remember an incident that took place some years ago which illustrates this point. I had been invited by a small church in West Texas to come and help dedicate their new building. While I was there, the pastor said he wanted to receive an offering for me and my wife, Carolyn.

He said, "Now I don't want this to go into your ministry; it will be for you two personally in appreciation of your work for the Lord and as an expression of our gratitude for what you have done for us in this church." The offering turned out to be $1,000.00.

Normally, all the offerings go directly to the ministry. I am on a set salary just like everyone else in the organization. Carolyn and I have to live within our income just as you do. So naturally it was a great joy and blessing to be able to bring in some extra cash just for our own use. In fact, in my mind I already had that money spent on several things we really needed.

But when I got home from that meeting, Carolyn met me at the door saying, "Jerry, there is a couple in town who are being evicted from their house. The movers are setting them and their children and their furniture out on the sidewalk right now. They have no money and no place to move. They don't know what they're going to do. They need a thousand dollars."

"Well, it just so happens that I have a thousand dollars on me," I replied. "When do they need it?" "Right now!" she said.

So we got in our car and drove over to the couple's house. The children were sitting out in the yard. The man and his wife were loading furniture into a trailer. It was about one o'clock in the morning, and they had no idea where they were going. They had no money and no place to even spend the night.

Then the Lord spoke to me and said, "This is the reason I gave you that thousand dollars. This is where I want it to go. That money will keep this family in their home."

I want to tell you something. Of all the things I could have bought for myself or my family with that thousand dollars, nothing could have brought me more happiness than that which I received in being the instrument of God to help that family in their time of need. There is no momentary thrill on earth that can ever compare with the deep, abiding joy of knowing that God has richly blessed you so you can be a blessing to others and prevent a misfortune or catastrophe in their lives.

Because of our willingness to pass on the blessings which God had freely bestowed upon us, that family was able to stay in their home. And God began to bless them and make them to be a blessing to our ministry as a result. They are partners in our outreach. They sow seed into our ministry all the time.

That is the real purpose of God's giving to us: to bless us and to make us channels of His blessing to others.

That is also why our giving is a grace - a free and undeserved gift from God. Because as we have seen, an opportunity to give to help others in need is really an opportunity to have our own needs met.

Reaping What You Sow

What am I saying? That we are going to have to stop being need-conscious and become seed-conscious.

If, like the Macedonian believers, you are in deep poverty, and if you are going through much trouble and hard times, the Devil will try to tell you that you cannot afford to give. If you believe that lie, and refuse to give to meet the needs of others and of God's work, you will cut yourself off from the very source of your own supply.

If you have great needs, never let Satan convince you that you can't afford to give. In order to receive, you must give; to reap, you must sow. And remember, you are not alone or unique in this respect. This is true of every Christian.

A few years ago, Carolyn and I were probably under the greatest financial pressure of our entire lives. Because of all the ministry projects and personal undertakings we were involved in, we had tremendous financial needs and obligations. At the time I delivered this message in that believers' convention, for example, we were involved in building a clinic in Kenya, building our new headquarters in Fort Worth and constructing a new home.

But God brought us through these and many other crucial times. The first phase of the clinic was completed and has begun treating, on the average, 125 people a day. The headquarters has been built and we are in our new home.

So I have needs - personal, professional, financial and spiritual - just as you do. But I have found that God is faithful; He always meets my needs. Usually the way He does that is by directing my attention away from my own needs to those of others. Instead of talking about my need, He speaks to me about my seed. He keeps telling me to give.

He says, "Plant a seed."

I am convinced that this is the way He is dealing with you too. But you have to be careful and not allow the Devil or other people to talk you out of your giving. Because that is the way you reap, by sowing. Now, I know you have heard that for years and years. Virtually every Christian church I know of preaches that same Biblical principle: *...whatsoever a man soweth, that shall he also reap.* Every true Christian leader knows that we reap what we sow. These believers to whom Paul was writing knew it too. But they had to be stirred up about it.

Carry Through to Completion

In 2 Corinthians 8:10,11 (TLB) Paul wrote to the church in Corinth:

I want to suggest that you finish what you started to do a year ago, for you were not only the first to propose this idea, but the first to begin doing something about it.

Having started the ball rolling so enthusiastically, you should carry this project through to completion just as gladly, giving whatever you can out of whatever you have. Let your enthusiastic idea at the start be equaled by your realistic action now.

Now that may describe your situation. You may have begun giving enthusiastically. You may have started the ball rolling well. But now you need to be stirred up to keep the "ball rolling," to finish what you started, to let your enthusiastic idea at the start be equaled by your realistic action now.

Satan's Purpose in Opposing the Spirit of Cheerful Giving

Don't let adverse circumstances, outside pressure or negative criticism pressure you into giving up on your giving. Remember, the Bible teaches that if you withhold your seed, it will tend to poverty.

That is exactly what Satan is trying to do to the Body of Christ today: to get Christians to withhold their seed. He is trying to use public ministry scandals to disturb, distress and discourage believers so they will withhold their giving to the Lord's work.

Now I am not ignoring the scandals, nor am I saying that there is no abuse or dishonesty or extremism in the ministry. These things always exist in the ministry. But the Devil will not call attention to the truth or the good. He will always dwell on the lies, the deceit and the wrong. He does that in order to cast doubt and to bring disruption and discouragement. He wants the Body of Christ to retreat from their position of godly prosperity and power, to draw back into the preaching and practice of the doctrine of poverty.

Satan's real goal and purpose is to render the Church of Jesus Christ weak and ineffective, unable to do anything because it doesn't have anything to do it with. He wants to keep it poor so it can never reach the nations of the world with the Gospel. The last thing Satan wants is for the Church to prosper because he knows that if it does, it will publish the Good News of Jesus Christ throughout the entire world. And that would spell the end for him and his kingdom of darkness.

God's Plan To Thwart Satan

Do you remember that the Bible says that the love of money is the root of all evil (1 Timothy 6:10)? Well, that is true. But it is Satan, not the Church, who is in love with money. He is the one who hoards it up for selfish purposes, not Christians. Satan's primary plan and goal is to accumulate all the wealth of the world so he can keep it away from the Church. Why? Because he knows that Christians will use riches, not to satisfy their own selfish, carnal desires, but to finance the spread and growth of God's Kingdom.

But God has already taken Satan's scheme into consideration and has made provision for it. He has declared that *...the wealth of the sinner* (the one the Devil "prospers") *has been laid up for the just* (Proverbs 13:22).

If we are faithful in giving to see God's will done on this earth, He has promised to "transfer" to us those funds collected and hoarded by Satan and his followers. That's part of the amazing plan of God - to thwart Satan's scheme for world conquest and dominion by taking his own evil resources and using them to finance the greatest revival the earth has ever known. *O the depth of the riches both of the wisdom and the knowledge of God!...* (Romans 11:33).

Sowing in Adversity

Giving whatever you can out of whatever you have...

If you are really eager to give, then it isn't important how much you give. God wants you to give what you have, not what you haven't.

2 Corinthians 8:11,12 (TLB)

If we in the Body of Christ wait for conditions to get just right before we give, we will never sow. And without sowing there will never be a harvest. No, like the early believers, you and I must learn to give out of our poverty, to sow in adversity, to plant seeds in the midst of our trouble.

Ecclesiastes 11:4 tells us: *He that observeth the wind shall not sow; and he that regardeth the clouds shall not reap.* The good farmer doesn't wait for perfect conditions. If he did, he would never sow nor reap a harvest. He has to exercise faith in God and faith in the seed he plants, even when they are sown under less than perfect conditions.

Whatever the prevailing circumstances, he is faithful to sow his seed. He expects that seed to do what it is capable of doing, what it is programmed to do - to reproduce bountifully after its own kind. He trusts in the never-failing miracle of the life-principle of sowing and reaping.

Paul told the Christians in Corinth that the Macedonians had given out of their poverty. He also said that they had mixed joy with their giving. They gave not only what they could afford, but much more. He testified that they did so, not because he had nagged them to give generously, but because they wanted to. He emphasized that they even went so far as to beg him to take their freewill gifts and offerings, so they could share in the joy of helping their brothers and sisters in Jerusalem (2 Corinthians 8:3, TLB). Best of all, Paul noted, they went beyond his highest hopes because they first gave of themselves to the Lord.

Then Paul reminds the Corinthians that they too had promised to give. In fact, they had been so enthusiastic about it that Paul was now sending Titus to them to encourage them to complete what they had begun. He called to their attention how many leaders there were in their midst, how much faith they had, how knowledgeable they were, how much love they had displayed for him and how much enthusiasm they had shown for the work of the Lord. Then he concluded by urging them to be ...*leaders also in the spirit of cheerful giving* (2 Corinthians 8:7 TLB).

As I have noted, I believe that in the days to come God is going to raise up leaders in our midst who have this same *spirit of cheerful giving.* The reason He is going to do that is so His people can have good examples and models to show them how to be blessed and how to become a blessing to many, many others.

Blessed to be a Blessing

I realize that I really don't even need to mention this to you, about helping God's people.

For I know how eager you are to do it, and I have boasted to the friends in Macedonia that you were ready to send an offering a year ago. In fact, it was this enthusiasm of yours that stirred up many of them to begin helping.

But I am sending these men just to be sure that you really are ready, as I told them you would be, with your money all collected; I don't want it to turn out that this time I was wrong in my boasting about you.

I would be very much ashamed - and so would you - if some of these Macedonian people come with me, only to find that you still aren't ready after all I have told them!

2 Corinthians 9:1-4 (TLB)

Here Paul is saying to the believers in Corinth that he has boasted of them to the Macedonians, emphasizing how eager they were to give to help God's people. He even says that it was their enthusiasm that had motivated the Macedonians to make their generous freewill gift. Now Paul wants to make sure that when he comes to collect the Corinthinans' offering, it will be there because they have followed through on their good intentions and fulfilled their promise. He wants to make sure that they have finished what they started.

So I have asked these other brothers to arrive ahead of me to see that the gift you promised is on hand and waiting. I want it to be a real gift and not look as if it were being given under pressure.

But remember this - if you give little, you will get little. A farmer who plants just a few seeds will get only a small crop, but if he plants much, he will reap much.

Every one must make up his own mind as to how much he should give. Don't force anyone to give more than he really wants to, for cheerful givers are the ones God prizes.

God is able to make it up to you by giving you everything you need and more, so that there will not only be enough for your own needs, but plenty left over to give joyfully to others.

Notice: Paul says that if we give, God will give us everything we need, and more, so we will have enough for our own needs and plenty left over to give joyfully to meet the needs of others.

That's the way God always operates. That is what He told Abraham in the first place: "Serve and obey Me, and you will be blessed, and will be a blessing to everyone else." You see, God's Covenant with us is twofold. If we are willing and obedient to Him, He has promised: first, to bless us personally, and, second, to make us to be a blessing to many, many others.

This means that as God's blessings come upon and overtake us, then we are able to pass those blessings on to meet the needs around us. We are not to be selfish with God's blessings. They are given to us so we can be a blessing to others in need.

So then, the expression "to be a blessing" actually means to be an instrument of God's divine favor. As I illustrated, it is such a blessing to be chosen to administer God's divine favor in the life of another person, preventing misfortune or catastrophe. There is no greater joy known to man. How wonderfully God has already blessed us, simply by choosing and anointing us to serve as His instruments of blessing to the world.

The problem is that so many people do not understand this principle. They think they should be blessed of God for their own sake alone, just to get their own needs met. They are only too happy to hear that they will have plenty left over - but for the wrong reason; they think it is to be used to satisfy their own selfish desires. As we have seen, that is not God's plan and purpose in blessing us.

It is selfish and unscriptural to pray and expect God to provide just enough to meet our own personal needs. It is even more selfish and unscriptural to pray and expect God to provide us wealth and riches to consume upon our own lusts. If you and I are going to be totally unselfish and truly scriptural, we must desire, pray and expect to receive from God not only enough to meet our own needs, but plenty left over so that we can give joyfully to help somebody else. That is God's plan. That is the Covenant.

The Purpose of Prosperity

I believe we are going to have to raise our level of thinking where prosperity is concerned. Too many of us are not yet on God's level of thought. To show you what I mean, let's look at that scripture which promises us that the wealth of the sinner is laid up for the just. That sounds like a marvelous promise to the believer - and it is - but let's examine the first part of that verse:

*A good man leaveth an inheritance to his children's children:
and the wealth of the sinner is laid up for the just.*

Proverbs 13:22

Now God's idea of prosperity is not just our having a
bare minimum, just enough to meet our own needs. To
God we are not fully prosperous until we have enough to
meet our current needs, plenty to give to meet the needs of
others, and then on top of that, enough left over to leave an
inheritance for two succeeding generations!

Now I surely don't mean to imply that I have reached
that level of divine prosperity yet. I haven't. Few
Christians have. But that doesn't mean that it is not available to us. I believe God wants to raise up some modern-
day, New Testament Abrahams. People who are blessed,
and who can be a blessing to "all the families of the earth."
Why not? If the heavyweight boxing champion of the
world can go into a ring and earn thirty-five million dollars
in ninety seconds, then surely God can find ways of supplying His children with enough riches to bless millions of
people around the globe.

But isn't it amazing that a prominent sports figure can
"earn" millions of dollars a year, and be made to look good
in the headlines? But if a preacher gets even so much as a
fine new car, he gets "headlines" of a very different sort!

But that really doesn't matter. The important thing is
that more and more of us are going to be blessed and prospered of the Lord in the days to come. That is all part of
God's overall plan for the salvation of the world. He is

going to "transfer" some of the wealth of the sinner to some of us (the righteous) so we can have the means to publish this Gospel throughout all the world - as He has expressly commanded us to do. Mark 16:15 says, *Go ye into all the world, and preach the gospel to every creature.*

There are millions of people who have yet to hear the old, old story. And you and I are responsible for getting it to them. God wants us to prosper. He wants us to be blessed. Of course, He doesn't want us to allow money to come between us and Him. But at the same time, He doesn't want us to get the mistaken idea that it is impossible to have money and still serve Him. Abraham had riches, and he served the Lord faithfully. So did Isaac. So did several others in Scripture.

Yes, the Bible does warn us about allowing material goods to interfere with our spirituality. The Bible does say that prosperity destroys fools (Proverbs 1:32). But you and I are not supposed to be fools, we are supposed to be wise sons and daughters of God. As children of the King, we ought to have sense enough to know how to handle our Father's estate.

Fools are destroyed by prosperity. But you and I have access to the mind and wisdom of God. We don't have to be foolish with prosperity, and thus be destroyed by it. We can use it wisely for God's purposes.

And the Bible indicates that if we are seed-minded rather than need-minded, God can trust us to handle His goods, knowing that they will be directed to those who need them most. He knows that we can be trusted to meet our own needs, and then to go on and give generously to meet the needs of those around us.

Look at what Paul says about God's purpose in prospering us:

For God, who gives seed to the farmer to plant, and later on, good crops to harvest and eat, will give you more and more seed to plant and will make it grow so that you can give away more and more fruit from your harvest.

Yes, God will give you much so that you can give away much...

2 Corinthians 9:10,11 (TLB)

Give Away and Become Richer

There is that scattereth, and yet increaseth; and there is that withholdeth more than is meet, but it tendeth to poverty. The liberal soul shall be made fat: and he that watereth shall be watered also himself.

Proverbs 11:24,25

This passage is so important to our study that I would like to look at it in three modern versions: **_The New International Version, The Living Bible_** and **_The Revised Standard Version:_**

NIV: *One man gives freely, yet gains even more; another withholds unduly, but comes to poverty. A generous man will prosper; he who refreshes others will himself be refreshed.*

TLB: *It is possible to give away and become richer! It is also possible to hold on too tightly and lose everything. Yes, the liberal man shall be rich! By watering others, he waters himself.*

RSV: *One man gives freely, yet grows all the richer; another withholds what he should give, and only suffers want. A liberal man will be enriched, and one who waters will himself be watered.*

You see, all this we are hearing these days about dishonesty and fraud in the media ministry is an attempt to get us to fall for the lie that we had better stop giving. Every day we hear voices that tell us: "Times are hard. You can't afford to give. Everything is shaky. You'd better hang on to what you have left, because who knows what is going to happen down the road. The economy is bad, the dollar is down, banks are closing right and left, the Dow Jones is falling."

All this is designed by the Devil to frighten and upset us, to scare us into withholding what we know we should give. The Devil is trying to convince people that withholding during hard times is "smart business." The Bible doesn't say it is smart, it says it is "dangerous business." It leads to poverty. It can cause us to lose everything. Remember: it is the one who refreshes others, who is himself refreshed.

Notice *The Living Bible* version of verse 24. I love it. It says that *it is possible to give away and become richer!* Now many people don't understand that principle. But it works. I know it does, because I have experienced the results of it in my own life. Let me show you what I mean.

Not long ago God told me to give away my airplane. (Actually I've given away several planes used in my ministry, but this story is just about one particular plane which the Lord instructed me to plant as seed into another ministry.) I gave it to the man the Lord indicated should receive it.

A few days later I came back home and was met by an airplane dealer who said to me, "Jerry, I'd like to make you an offer on that plane of yours. I've got a nice one that is just a bit larger and nicer than what you're flying now."

Before I could answer, he went on, "You know what this plane is worth. Well, I'm going to knock sixty thousand dollars off the purchase price right up front. Then I'm going to give you fifty thousand dollars more for your present plane than what you can sell it for. So actually I'm going to take your old plane and allow you more than a hundred thousand dollar discount on the larger one."

That was wonderful. There was just one problem, of course. I had just given away my plane the night before. I listened very politely to the man's offer. Then he asked me,

"What do you think of the deal?"

"Well, that's a very generous offer," I told him. "I really appreciate it. But there is just one problem."

"What's that?" he wanted to know.

"I just gave my plane away."

Now this man was not a believer, so he really didn't understand much about this spiritual principle of giving and receiving, sowing and reaping.

"You're lying," he replied. "Here you are a preacher, and you're lying. Nobody gives away an airplane."

"I did," I answered.

"Yeah, well, I'm in the airplane business, and I've never heard of such a thing."

"That may be," I responded, "but I did it anyway. In fact, that's how I got that plane in the first place; somebody gave it to me. I gave away another one, and then someone gave me that one."

"I don't understand that," the man muttered. "Nobody goes around giving away airplanes."

"Oh yes, some of us do," I assured him. "There's a whole bunch of us around the country who do that very thing. That's how we live - we give."

The man walked away, shaking his head in wonder and disbelief.

The Choice Is Yours

But notice that not only does this passage say that it is possible to give away and grow richer, it also says that *it is possible to hold on too tightly and lose everything.* That's sort of the "flip side" of the equation.

Well, if that is so, I think it would be wise to be a "liberal soul." Because the Bible says that it is the liberal man who will be enriched.

Now that does not mean that you and I are to go "hog wild" and give away everything we own, under the false impression that we are going to immediately get it all back a hundred times over! No, I am not telling you that. But I am telling you that it would be good to start giving to the Lord's work as He leads and instructs you to give - wisely.

Learn to listen to the voice of the Lord, and then do what He tells you to do in this area of giving. Or you can listen to the Devil. If you do, he will tell you that times are hard and getting harder. He will warn you that you'd better hold back on giving until "things get better." So you have a choice: you can choose to listen to the Lord or to the Devil.

Isn't it amazing how the Lord is always giving us choices? In the Old Testament, He told the children of Israel that He was setting before them blessing or cursing, and that it was their decision which they would choose. But He also urged them to choose life, so that they and their families might live (Deuteronomy 30:19,20).

I believe that is the choice God is setting before you and me today. And I believe He is urging us to choose life, so that we and our families might live through the difficult days which lie ahead of us all.

The choice is yours. I urge you to choose life.

The Decision Is Crucial

My friend, I sincerely believe that the Spirit of God is saying to His Church that there are some troubled days ahead. Hard times are coming. The world is not yet through being shaken.

But the Lord says that you and I can rule and reign, regardless of the circumstances of life. God has promised that whatever lies ahead for the world, you and I can not only survive, but even grow richer. We can have the upper hand.

He has made provision for us to do just that. How? He has called us to become seed-minded instead of need-minded.

3

GIVING PRODUCES RECEIVING

3

GIVING PRODUCES RECEIVING

Cast thy bread upon the waters: for thou shalt find it after many days.

Give a portion to seven, and also to eight: for thou knowest not what evil shall be upon the earth.

If the clouds be full of rain, they empty themselves upon the earth: and if the tree fall toward the south, or toward the north, in the place where the tree falleth, there it shall be.

He that observeth the wind shall not sow; and he that regardeth the clouds shall not reap.

And thou knowest not what is the way of the spirit, nor how the bones do grow in the womb of her that is with child: even so thou knowest not the works of God who maketh all.

In the morning sow thy seed, and in the evening withhold not thine hand: for thou knowest not whether shall prosper, either this or that, or whether they both shall be alike good.

Ecclesiastes 11:1-6

This passage of Scripture is so important to a full and clear understanding of godly giving, that I would like for us to read it again, this time in *The Living Bible* translation:

Give generously, for your gifts will return to you later.

Divide your gifts among many, for in the days ahead you your-self may need much help.

When the clouds are heavy, the rains come down; when a tree falls, whether south or north, the die is cast, for there it lies.

If you wait for perfect conditions, you will never get anything done.

God's ways are as mysterious as the pathway of the wind, and as the manner in which a human spirit is infused into the little body of a baby while it is yet in its mother's womb.

Keep on sowing your seed, for you never know which will grow - perhaps it all will.

Now in this passage we see a vital principle of godly giv-ing; "Give generously, for your gifts will return to you later."

Now some people may say, "I just don't believe that." Well, whether this principle is believed or not does not change the truth of it. It just affects whether or not it works for you.

There is a little slogan going around these days which you may have seen on bumper stickers: "God said it, I believe it, that settles it!" The truth is, if God has said it, it is already settled, whether you or I or anybody else believes it or not. Our believing it is to our advantage.

God's Mysterious Ways

You might say to me, "I just don't understand how I can give away something and expect God to give it back to me."

I know you don't understand that. Neither do I. That's what this passage means when it says that God's ways are as mysterious as the pathway of the wind, and as the manner in which a human spirit is infused into the little body of a baby while it is yet in its mother's womb. Of course, we don't understand how such things happen; we just know they do.

It is not necessary that we understand God's principles to benefit from them. We must simply learn them, believe them, and act upon them.

For example, we don't know how seeds bring forth plants or fruit. We just know they do, so we sow seeds into the ground, patiently tend and nurture them, and then reap an abundant harvest from them. That's what God expects us to do with the good seed of His Word.

I don't understand how the Lord can tell me to plant a seed-gift in the ministry of another man of God, and then provide me in return a generous gift from someone else who lives in California - someone I don't even know! I may be in Illinois, and the next thing you know I meet someone from California who has been sent there by the Lord for the express purpose of sowing a seed-gift into my life and ministry.

I don't know how that sort of thing happens, I just know it does, time and time again.

As for this particular incident, I was in a church in the state of Illinois for a series of meetings. I preached seven sermons without receiving a single offering for my ministry because the Lord spoke to me and told me not to accept an offering.

"You know, Father," I pointed out to Him, "I do have a budget to meet."

But still, I was obedient. I did as I was told to do. I preached all week long without receiving an offering. After the meetings were over, I left town.

On my way back home to Texas, I stopped to speak at a Full Gospel Business Men's banquet. As I began to prepare for the service, the Lord again spoke to me and said, "Don't take an offering here either."

From there, I was scheduled to drive the rest of the way home. After a while, I stopped off the freeway to have lunch. I walked into a restaurant and looked for a place to sit down. Now I didn't walk in carrying a huge Bible or wearing a sign proclaiming that I was Jerry Savelle, "the great man of God." I wasn't even wearing a suit and tie. I had on comfortable, traveling clothes like everyone else there.

Now you must realize that this was a good 20 years ago, and not too many people had ever heard of me. But after I sat down and ordered my meal, an elderly couple got up from their table, came over, and politely tapped me on the shoulder.

"You don't know us, but we know who you are," they told me. "We were sitting over there talking about you before you came in a while ago."

Then the lady told me, "I said to my husband, 'Why, that's Jerry Savelle right there, isn't it?' And he said, 'You know, I believe it is.'"

They went on to tell me that before I had entered the room, the Lord had spoken to them about giving me an offering. They had already decided to mail it to me at my office in Fort Worth as soon as they got back home. But the Lord told them that would be too late. Just then, they saw me walk in. The Lord immediately instructed them to give the offering to me in person, right then and there. That generous offering was more than enough to cover the expenses of that meeting with some left over.

Now I don't know how God does that kind of thing. I don't understand it, but that's not my responsibility. My responsibility is to plant the seed. It is God's responsibility to meet the need.

If you and I become "need-conscious," we won't be "seed-conscious." If we get to thinking we have so many needs we just can't afford to plant seeds, we will soon be right. If we don't sow in time of need, those needs are going to increase so much we really won't have anything to sow, and therefore nothing to harvest. Remember the principle: "Withholding more than is right tends to poverty."

It is our job to sow seeds, God's job to meet needs.
But notice that the Bible says only that our godly gifts will come back to us; it doesn't say how or when. I wish I could tell you how or when your gift will be returned to you in multiplied form. I don't know. If God gives me a word of wisdom for you, I will let you know, of course. But until such time, all I can do is pass on to you the spiritual principle: "Godly giving results in abundant receiving."

How much time will elapse between our sowing and reaping, I simply do not know. But I do know one thing: the time between sowing and reaping is the most important and exciting in our lives; it becomes a great adventure in faith. The secret is to sow faithfully, generously and regularly, so that we can expect a continual flow of godly gifts in return.

Divide Your Gifts

Notice that verse 2 of the passage from Ecclesiastes 11 (TLB) says, *Divide your gifts among many, for in the days ahead you yourself may need help.*

What is God saying to us here? He is trying to prepare us for the future, for whatever may be coming down the road. If things are tough now, if we are having a hard time making it through these days, then how will we ever be able to face even worse times to come?

From all indications, world conditions are not going to improve in the future; they are going to continue to worsen. But that doesn't mean that the Body of Christ has to be overcome by the world and its failing economic and social order. Just because the world's system is failing, there is no reason that the Church of Jesus Christ must go under. If anything, the failure of the world's system should herald the greatest resurgence and revival of the Church in the history of mankind.

I believe that what God really desires is, when the world is at its worst, the Church is to be at its best. The world's darkest hour will be the Church's brightest hour. That is what the prophet Isaiah was referring to when he told the people of his day:

Arise, shine; for thy light is come, and the glory of the Lord is risen upon thee.

For, behold, the darkness shall cover the earth, and gross darkness the people: but the Lord shall arise upon thee, and his glory shall be seen upon thee.

And the Gentiles shall come to thy light, and kings to the brightness of thy rising.

Isaiah 60:1-3

But the days ahead will not be our brightest hour if we withhold our giving. Without sowing into God's kingdom, we will end up as dark as the world; The Lord has instructed us to "divide" our gifts - to sow them - among many, so we will have "much help" in the days to come.

Remember: God's ways are not man's ways; in that sense, they are "mysterious." Keep on sowing, for you never know which of your seeds will grow and produce an abundant harvest. Maybe they all will.

You may have planted and sowed, day in and day out, for weeks or even months, with no apparent results. Don't get discouraged. How do you know that today is not the appointed day of harvest? How do you know that the next seed you sow is not the very one that will cause all the other seeds to come to fruition?

Divide your seed among many, and then expect to harvest a "many-fold" return on your sowing.

Be Consistent in Giving

Some time ago, I was talking to the International Director of our ministry in Africa. We were discussing the battle royal we had gone through in that land. At every step we had to battle corruption and opposition. But God had told us to go into that area and pull down the strongholds of Satan, and that was exactly what we intended to do, troubles or no troubles.

Our loyal workers lived under constant threat, in turmoil and stress, twenty-four hours a day, with never a moment to relax. They were never able to let down their guard for an instant. The warfare they were engaged in was not only spiritual but also natural.

Some people were so opposed to the ministry, they had actually hired assassins to kill the members of our staff. But despite the dangers, obstacles and opposition from both man and Satan, we just kept on planting seeds into that outreach, week after week, month after month. After nine long months of seeming failure, we finally began to see a return on our investment in those precious African lives.

Now my director tells me that he and his staff can hardly contain their joy because every day brings a new victory over the forces of evil and darkness. All the seed we had been faithfully and consistently planting, suddenly began to grow and produce fruit for the Kingdom of God.

So don't become discouraged and quit sowing. Don't stop planting seed just because you don't see any immediate results.

Don't be like the man who heard that God rewards the tither. He began to tithe faithfully, but when he didn't see any returns on his tithes within three weeks, He concluded that it didn't work and stopped giving. He lost everything he had sown because he gave up too soon. He expected to harvest as soon as he planted. Don't make that mistake. Keep planting those seeds. You will reap "in due season" (Galatians 6:9).

The Law of Refreshing

There is that scattereth, and yet increaseth; and there is that withholdeth more than is meet, but it tendeth to poverty. The liberal soul shall be made fat: and he that watereth shall be watered also himself.

Proverbs 11:24,25

Remember *The New International Version* translates verse 25 of this passage: *A generous man will prosper; he who refreshes others will himself be refreshed.*

Now this concept was not thought up by a few preachers who go around the country preaching prosperity. Modern-day man didn't write these words; they were written centuries ago under the inspiration of the Holy Spirit. This is not my plan and promise; it is God's plan and promise.

The concept is simple: God has decreed that the person who refreshes others through his gift-giving will himself be similarly refreshed. Verse 24 in *The New International Version* states that it is possible to give freely and yet gain even more. Giving is always a refreshment, and those who refresh others with their material goods will themselves be refreshed by the Lord.

If you will refresh others, God will see to it that you are refreshed. If your attitude is "nobody ever gives me anything," then you should know why that is true in your life. It's because you don't give anything to anybody else. You are reaping what you sow.

Some people tell me, "Well, when I need money, I don't give, I just work, work, work."

I also believe that Christians ought to work. God believes that too. In fact, it was His idea. The Bible clearly teaches this spiritual principle. In 1 Timothy 5:8 Paul went so far as to say that ...*if any provide not for his own, and specially for those of his own house, he hath denied the faith, and is worse than an infidel.*

In 2 Thessalonians 3:10 he writes: *For even when we were with you, this we commanded you, that if any would not work, neither should he eat.*

Finally, in 1 Thessalonians 4:11,12 (NIV), Paul reminds his readers: *Make it your ambition to lead a quiet life, to mind your own business and to work with your hands, just as we told you, so that your daily life may win the respect of outsiders and so that you will not be dependent on anybody.*

The Bible indicates that the reason we should work is so we will not be dependent on others, but will have seed to sow in the lives of those about us in need. As we have already noted, as Christians, you and I do not work for a living, we work for a giving.

This passage in Proverbs assures us that it is possible to give away and grow richer. The world doesn't understand that principle. They say it is impossible. But Jesus said ...*the things which are impossible with men are possible with God* (Luke 18:27). The world says to get all you can, and then hold on to it. God says just the opposite; He says to give.

If you will keep on giving, faithfully and consistently, to refresh others, the Lord will see to it that you are refreshed in turn. He has promised it. I urge you to act on that word of promise.

Seven Results of Godly Giving

Bring ye all the tithes into the storehouse, that there may be meat in mine house, and prove me now herewith, saith the Lord of hosts, if I will not open you the windows of heaven, and pour you out a blessing, that there shall not be room enough to receive it.

Malachi 3:10

In this familiar passage, the Lord has revealed to us seven results of godly giving. Let's look at them one at a time:

1. Giving releases our faith in the faithfulness of God.

Did you know that giving is an act of faith? When we give of our material means, especially what we need to live on, it releases our faith in God and in His absolute faithfulness. If we didn't believe that God is faithful to His Word, which promises to reward us richly for our giving, then we would be tempted to withhold our gifts for our own use.

Perhaps that's why so many Christians hold back from giving freely: they are afraid of losing what they give away, what they need so desperately. They have no real faith that God will keep His Word and meet their every need, in accordance with His riches in glory, as He has promised (Philippians 4:19).

2. Giving establishes God's Covenant in our lives.

The Covenant which God made with Abraham in the

Old Testament also applies to us today. We have seen that because of his faith, Abraham was promised by God that He would bless him, and make him to be a blessing to "all the families of the earth." These blessings also were pronounced upon the seed (the offspring) of Abraham forever. We saw that because of what Jesus Christ has done for us, you and I, as seed (offspring) of Abraham, have been freed from the curse of the Law and restored to our rightful position as sons and daughters of God. As such, we are heirs to the promises God made to Abraham, heirs to the Covenant.

The way you and I establish (or ratify) the Covenant in our own individual lives is by acting upon the provisions of it. By our faithful, obedient giving, in response to God's command, we activate the provisions of that Covenant which guarantees that we will be blessed with the same blessing God poured out upon our spiritual ancestor, Abraham.

There are many children of God who are not enjoying Covenant privileges and provision. The reason is because they are ignorant of their Covenant, or else they are afraid to establish it in their own lives by freely giving. I hope that you are learning not to be one of those people. The Covenant worked for Abraham in his day, and it will work for you too in your time.

3. Giving links us to the highest authority in the universe.

God has promised that when we give of our tithes and offerings to Him and His work, He will open to us the windows of heaven and pour us out such an abundant blessing that we won't be able to contain it. Notice Who does the pouring out: God Himself. We don't have to look to men to meet our needs, though God will use people in that role; but it will be God Himself Who undertakes to bless us and to make us to become a blessing to many, many others.

Our giving puts us into contact and Covenant with the Supreme Power of the Universe, Who cannot and will not fail.

4. Giving releases the power of God on our behalf.

As we have said, God has promised that when we tithe, He will do something for us in return. One of the things He does is to open the windows of heaven and pour us out a blessing in abundance. *The New International Version* translates this verse:

Bring the whole tithe into the storehouse, that there may be food in my house. Test me in this, says the Lord Almighty, and see if I will not throw open the floodgates of heaven and pour you out so much blessing that you will not have room enough for it.

Thus, it is clear that, by our giving, the power of God is released on our behalf. Our giving literally opens to us the floodgates of heaven.

5. Giving enlarges our capacity to receive from God.

Isn't this what the Lord is saying to us in Malachi 3:10? That if we will bring the whole tithe into His storehouse, and put Him to the test in our giving, He will pour us out an overflowing blessing? Why the overflow? So we will have not only enough for our own needs, but plenty left over to give to others (2 Corinthians 9:11 TLB).

The best part is that, as we continue to give, we continue to increase in our ability to receive. The more we give, the greater our return. The greater our return, the larger our tithe. The larger our tithe, the larger our return. It just keeps growing and growing, in an ever-increasing cycle of giving, receiving and blessing - for ourselves and for many others.

Now don't get the idea that we give just to get. That's a wrong emphasis. We don't really give to get, instead we get to give. We have said that we work and invest so we will reap an abundant harvest, that is true. But we do that, not so we will have an abundance of things to fulfill our selfish desires, but so we will have seed to invest in God's work and give to others to meet their needs.

Nor do we give out of a sense of obligation. Instead, we give because we want to give - because we sincerely want to be a blessing to others, just as much as we want to be blessed.

Many years ago I heard Oral Roberts say that he had long ago gotten out of the realm of obligation and into the realm of faith. He said that the tithe is not a debt we owe, but a seed we sow. I like that concept: "Freely we have received, so freely we give."

The best part of that concept is that it doesn't end there. The more freely we give, the more freely we receive; but the opposite is also true, the more freely we receive, the more freely we give: ...*not grudgingly, or of necessity* (out of obligation): *for God loveth a cheerful giver* (2 Corinthians 9:7).

The reason God loves a cheerful giver is because He Himself is a cheerful giver. The Bible teaches us that God takes pleasure in the prosperity (well-being) of His servants (Psalms 35:27). It also teaches us that God is love (1 John 4:16). And love gives. If you and I love to give, it is because we are the sons and daughters of our heavenly Father, Whose very nature is that of selfless, loving giving.

Giving is what Christianity is all about. If Christians were acting like Christians, there would be no needs in the Body of Christ. If every believer went through his day asking the Lord to show him where to plant seed into His work, the results would be staggering. Every need could be met. And the return on that giving would produce such an abundant harvest that we would have the means to publish the Gospel around the world to those who have not yet heard.

Can you imagine the impact on this world if God's people became truly "seed-conscious?" It would increase our ability to receive so greatly that we would ultimately be able to finance the greatest revival in the history of the Church!

6. Giving increases our capacity to receive more of God Himself.

There was a certain man in Caesarea called Cornelius, a centurion of the band called the Italian band.

A devout man, and one that feared God with all his house, which gave much alms to the people, and prayed to God alway.

He saw in a vision evidently about the ninth hour of the day an angel of God coming in to him, and saying unto him, Cornelius.

And when he looked on him, he was afraid, and said, What is it, Lord? And he said unto him, Thy prayers and thine alms are come up for a memorial before God.

Acts 10:1-4

The Living Bible translation of verse 4 says, *...Your prayers and charities have not gone unnoticed by God!*

You remember that we have said that God prizes cheerful givers. Because Cornelius was such a cheerful giver, his giving did not go unnoticed by the Lord.

What was the result of this man's giving?

Because he was obedient and sent for Simon Peter, as he was instructed by the angel of the Lord, Cornelius and his whole household received the Spirit of the Living God. They were the first Gentiles to be granted the salvation of the Lord. But they were not the last, not by any means. God used this faithful man to usher in a new movement, the coming of the Holy Spirit upon all Gentiles.

That tells me that my giving, like that of Cornelius, enlarges my capacity to receive not only more from God but also more of God.

Our giving reveals that we want more from God and more of God in our lives. It also shows that we are willing to take something that belongs to us and invest it freely into God's Kingdom. That action indicates to God that we are ready for greater authority and responsibility.   It also provides us the capacity to receive more from Him and of Him.

7. Giving increases the fruits of our righteousness.

Now he that ministereth seed to the sower both minister bread for your food, and multiply your seed sown, and increase the fruits of your righteousness.

2 Corinthians 9:10

In this verse we are told that our giving results in an increase in the fruits of our righteousness. What are the "fruits of righteousness?"

And the work of righteousness shall be peace; and the effect of righteousness quietness and assurance for ever.

And my people shall dwell in a peaceable habitation, and in sure dwellings, and in quiet resting places.

Isaiah 32:17,18

In our next chapter, we will be looking in detail at the four fruits of righteousness which are increased by our giving. Right now, just let me point out that this passage simply means that when we give to the Lord and His work, He guarantees us freedom from fear, anxiety, worry, stress, unrest and loss of sleep. Instead we live in peace and assurance, in peaceable habitations, in sure dwellings, in quiet resting places.

We still don't know how or when our promised return will be manifested, but we know it will be. We wait on the Lord in quietness of spirit and assurance of heart because we know that He is "faithful who has promised" (Hebrews 11:11). We remain in complete calm and tranquillity because, like the prophet Isaiah, we know that this is the inheritance of the servants of the Lord, and that our right-eousness is of Him (Isaiah 54:17).

God's Solution for Need

And there was a famine in the land, beside the first famine that was in the days of Abraham...

And the Lord appeared unto him (Isaac), and said, Go not down into Egypt; dwell in the land which I shall tell thee of:

Sojourn in this land, and I will be with thee, and will bless thee; for unto thee, and unto thy seed, I will give all these countries, and I will perform the oath which I sware unto Abraham thy father;

Then Isaac sowed in that land, and received in the same year an hundredfold: and the Lord blessed him.

Genesis 26:1-3,12

Here we see that while many others were seeking refuge from the famine by fleeing to Egypt, Isaac was instructed by the Lord to stay in the land and sow in the midst of famine.

The result of his obedience was a hundredfold return on what he sowed.

That is God's solution to financial famine. Not to withhold, but to give, to sow in time of adversity. Once again we see that God is seed-minded, not need-minded. I believe that is the way you and I are going to come out of our financial crisis: by remaining in the land of promise and faithfully sowing in time of famine.

Do you remember the incident that took place at the table during the Last Supper? Jesus knew that Judas was making plans to betray Him to the Jews. During the meal, He turned to him and said, "What you must do, do quickly" (John 13:27). The disciples heard this exchange between them, but thought that since Judas kept the money bag, Jesus was instructing him to go and give money to someone in need. Obviously Jesus had a reputation for giving.

That is the kind of reputation the Lord wants you and me to have as His children. He has promised that as we remain "in the land," (in Him and in His Word and will), He will provide for us a multiplied return, a bountiful blessing, if we are faithful and obedient enough to continue to sow in time of famine.

4

GIVING AS A LIFESTYLE

4

GIVING AS A LIFESTYLE

As we saw several times in Chapter 3, the Lord promises us in Malachi 3:10 that if we will be faithful in our tithes and offerings, He will open to us the windows of heaven and pour us out an abundant blessing.

The Lamsa translation quotes this passage: *I will open the windows of heaven for you and pour out blessings for you until you shall say, It is enough!* Now I don't know about you, but I haven't yet been so blessed by the Lord that I have had to shout, "Stop Lord, that's enough!"

We also saw that in *The New International Version* the expression "windows of heaven" is translated as "floodgates of heaven." Can you imagine God literally flooding us with blessings?

Now I know something about what it is like to be flooded, completely inundated. Several years ago my family and I were the victims of a flash flood in our neighborhood. It rained so hard it was almost unbelievable. The wind was blowing like a hurricane. It forced the rain to fall at an angle so that it came right through the cracks around the windows and doors in our house.

The rainwater started running down the walls and soaking the furniture and carpets, so I ran to get a mop. But the water was coming in faster than I could clean it up. I kept trying to sweep and mop up the rising water, but it was no use; I couldn't contain it. Finally I got so tired and frustrated that I just sat down on the floor, in all that water and ruined carpet, and began to laugh.

As I sat there, soaking wet, laughing to myself, I thought of the verse about God blessing in such abundance that it could not be contained. Suddenly the Lord spoke to me and said, "Now this is how I want My blessings to come down upon you." I got the message. Now I want you to get it - and the blessings that go with it.

I must admit that I don't know many people who have yet been blessed so much that they have had to shout, "It is enough!" But that doesn't mean that such blessings are not available to us as Christians. God has said that He will provide a flood of blessings for those of us who will be faithful in our tithing and giving. I believe it is God's will and desire to bless us with just such an overflowing abundance because it is part of His plan for reaching the whole world with the Gospel of Jesus Christ.

Giving is a Lifestyle - Not an Experiment

When the Lord told the children of Israel to "prove" Him, to "put Him to the test" in this area of giving, He did not mean that to be a one-time incident. He meant that if they were continually faithful to him in their tithing and giving, He would be continually faithful to them in His abundant, overflowing provision for their needs.

What God is asking us to do is to make godly giving a lifestyle - not just an experiment. Many people try this principle for a few weeks, then if they don't see immediate results, they decide it doesn't work, and give up. When the overflowing blessing doesn't appear instantly, they quit giving. They don't understand that this is a lifestyle to be adopted and maintained.

Several years ago I wrote a book entitled **Giving: the Essence of Living.** That title says it all. That's what living is all about - giving. A lot of people live their whole lives "on the take," always trying to get something for nothing. That is not the lifestyle Jesus introduced into this world. The Christian lifestyle is one of giving.

Jesus told His disciples: *Greater love hath no man than this, that a man lay down his life for his friends* (John 15:13). Now the expression "lay down his life," in this verse, does not always mean to die. To "lay down your life" for another person means to put the other person's will, desire, and well-being ahead of your own. To do that, you don't necessarily have to die physically. You simply have to be willing to dedicate your life to working for that person's welfare and benefit, rather than for your own. Jesus says that kind of unselfish giving of oneself is the greatest love known to man. It is the lifestyle which He introduced, displayed and modeled for us, and it is the kind of lifestyle He calls us to adopt.

Remember when the rich young ruler came to Jesus asking what he had to do to inherit eternal life? Jesus told him to go and sell everything he had, give the money to the poor, and then come and follow Him as His disciple. What was He introducing to that young man? A new lifestyle, a lifestyle of giving.

Jesus wasn't telling that young fellow, "I'm sorry, I can't help you because you're rich. You see, you must be poor in order to enter the kingdom of heaven." No, He wasn't saying that at all. He did say that it is hard for those who trust in riches to enter the kingdom of God (Mark 10:24). But why is that? Because their trust is in their wealth, not in the One Who provided that wealth.

Also notice that Jesus did not say that it is impossible for the rich to enter the kingdom, only that it is hard. I know many rich people who are having no difficulty at all in serving God. They simply trust in Him instead of in their riches. No matter how rich a person becomes, there are always situations, circumstances and influences beyond the power of money to control. No one, no matter how wealthy, is immune to the need for the living God.

Jesus taught a lifestyle of giving. Many people, even many Christians, do not understand this simple truth. That is the reason I am bringing the Body of Christ this important word from the Lord. My purpose in preaching this message in that convention and in publishing it in this book is not to tell anyone how to "get rich quick!" If anyone receives this message and thinks that what I am preaching is "all you have to do is give and God will make you rich," he is very much mistaken. I am not talking about getting, I am talking about giving - about an entire lifestyle of giving.

Long ago I made the decision that I am going to serve the Lord whether or not I ever get any better off financially. If I never see a financial miracle, if I never have a better car, if I never get a nicer house, if I am never prospered one bit more than I am today, I am still going to serve the Lord. Whatever the consequences, I will continue to "lay down my life" for Him and for the sake of His kingdom and people. Why? Because I am motivated, not by a love for things, but by a consuming love for God and the creatures made in His image.

But Jesus has said that those who seek first the kingdom of God and His righteousness will be rewarded by the Lord (Matt. 6:33). All the things they need (not all the things they lust after) will be added to them.

For the past twenty-five years I have been seeking the Lord and His kingdom and righteousness, and for the past twenty-five years I have been blessed by God. I can't help it if I am blessed. Everywhere I go, there is a godly blessing just waiting to "come on me." Is that so strange, so hard to believe? After all, didn't the Lord say that if we were faithful, His blessings would pursue us and overtake us?

God's Promises to the Giver

In several passages in the Bible, the Lord has made precious promises to those of us who are godly givers - those who obey His commandments, bring their tithes and offerings into the storehouse, and give in other ways as directed by God. Let's look at three of these promises:

1. God's blessings will come on us and overtake us.

And it shall come to pass, if thou shalt hearken diligently unto

*the voice of the Lord thy God, to observe and to do all his com-
mandments which I command thee this day, that the Lord thy God
will set thee on high above all nations of the earth:*

*And all these blessings shall come on thee, and overtake thee, if
thou shalt hearken unto the voice of the Lord thy God.*

Deuteronomy 28:1,2

A while back I was out jogging and as I came upon and
passed an 80 year old man the significance of this passage
suddenly struck me. In the same way that I overtook that
elderly man, so the blessings of the Lord will come upon
and overtake us - if we are careful to obey the will and Word
of the Lord.

2. *God will rebuke the devourer for our sakes.*

*And I will rebuke the devourer for your sakes, and he shall not
destroy the fruits of your ground; neither shall your vine cast her
fruit before the time in the field, saith the Lord of hosts.*

Malachi 3:11

According to the New Testament, you and I have the
power and authority to cast out demons (Mark 16:17). We
have discovered that this is an effective and powerful way
to keep Satan and his demons from taking from us the
health, wealth and blessings Christ died to provide for us,
our rightful inheritance as heirs of God and joint-heirs with
Christ. We know too that Jesus has delegated to us the
power and authority to bind and loose on earth (Mark
16:19). This is also a tremendous blessing and privilege.

But as marvelous as those blessings are, here in this Old Testament passage God assures us that if we will be faithful in our tithes and offerings, He Himself will rebuke the devourer (Satan) for us, for our sakes. In Chapter 3 we saw that it is our giving which releases the mighty power of God on our behalf. Here now we see exactly what that power does for us: it frees us from the power of Satan and protects us against his attempts to steal, kill and destroy. *...If God be for us, who can be against us?* (Romans 8:31).

3. God will increase our storehouse of seed.

For God, who gives seed to the farmer to plant, and later on, good crops to harvest and eat, will give you more and more seed to plant and will make it grow so that you can give away more and more fruit from your harvest.

2 Corinthians 9:10 (TLB)

Here Paul assures us that if we follow a consistent lifestyle of giving, the Lord will see to it that our storehouse of seed is continually replenished. Why? So we will have more and more seed to invest, to produce more and more fruit. For what purpose? So we can live in luxury and ease while the rest of the world goes hungry? No! So we will have more and more fruit to give away, to meet the needs of others.

That's the Christian lifestyle: giving and receiving, being blessed to be a blessing, prospering for the sake of all those in need.

Increasing the Fruits of Righteousness

Remember in the last chapter, we discussed a promise of the Lord to those believers who give: our giving results in an increase in the fruits of our righteousness according to 1 Corinthians 9:10:

Now he that ministereth seed to the sower both minister bread for your food, and multiply your seed sown, and increase the fruits of your righteousness.

In Isaiah 32:17 and 28 we see at least four "fruits of righteousness."

And the work of righteousness shall be peace; and the effect of righteousness quietness and assurance for ever.

And my people shall dwell in a peaceable habitation, and in sure dwellings, and in quiet resting places.

Let's look at this important passage in the *New International Version:*

The fruit of righteousness will be peace; the effect of righteousness will be quietness and confidence forever.

My people will live in peaceful dwelling places, in secure homes, in undisturbed places of rest.

1. Peace

As you and I become faithful and consistent godly givers, our lifestyle of giving actually begins to create an atmosphere of peace in us and around us. This is particularly true, and especially important, during times of adversity, when the economy is bad, when things are falling apart. When "all hell breaks loose," people will naturally be drawn to those who manifest the "peace of God."

This peace will come upon us and overtake us because we are linked to the God of all peace and are living in harmony with Him.

2. Quietness

When he (the Lord) *giveth quietness, who then can make trouble?...*

Job 34:29

According to Isaiah 32:17,18, one "effect" of the work of righteousness is quietness of spirit.

If there has ever been a time in the history of the Church when people everywhere have needed and hungered for quietness of spirit, it is now. With all the turmoil, harassment and adversity that the Body of Christ has recently experienced, what a wonderful blessing it would be to possess quietness of spirit.

With this God-given sense of quietness, you and I can lie down at night knowing that all of our needs are being pro-

vided for us. We can be at ease in our minds and hearts.
Not just occasionally. Not just when things are going well,
when the economy is on the upswing, when the stock mar-
ket is rising, but at all times, regardless of our outward circumstances.

3. Confidence

*And this is the confidence that we have in him, that, if we ask
any thing according to his will, he heareth us:*

*And if we know that he hear us, whatsoever we ask, we know
that we have the petitions that we desired of him.*

1 John 5:14,15

*And having this confidence, I know that I shall abide and con-
tinue...*

Philippians 1:25

Although I have needs, just as everyone else does, I also
have something that not everyone else possesses - a sense of
confidence. Confidence in the Lord, and confidence in my
own well-being. Despite my problems, I am still absolutely
convinced that God will meet my needs in accordance with
His riches in glory through Jesus Christ my Lord.

Many times I meet other people who are experiencing
need, and I sympathize with them because I know what it
is to be in that situation. Often I will give to them because
I know their need is great and the pressure is getting to
them. I also know that by giving to them I am taking action

toward fulfilling my own lack. I have a deep-seated confidence in my giving, because I am persuaded that the Lord will return my gift to me somehow, some way, because He is faithful. So by giving I am actually helping to meet both of our needs, the other person's and my own.

4. Assurance

...whereof he hath given assurance unto all men...

Acts 17:31

I don't know how many times Carolyn and I have had a great need, and then received from the Lord the very amount necessary to meet that obligation. Almost invariably, before we could use that money to settle our debt, we would come into contact with someone else whose financial need was even more pressing than ours - with one difference. We would realize that we knew something the other person didn't know. We knew how to believe and receive from the Lord; he or she didn't.

Many are the times we have given away to someone else what we ourselves desperately needed. How could we do that? How could we put the needs of others ahead of our own? We could do that only because we had a God-given assurance that by meeting the needs of others, we were guaranteeing that our own needs would be met by the Lord.

Carolyn and I know that God will meet our needs. We are fully persuaded. He has done it for us so many times before, how could we ever doubt Him?

Joy Comes From Giving

They that sow in tears shall reap in joy. He that goeth forth and weepeth, bearing precious seed, shall doubtless come again with rejoicing, bringing his sheaves with him.

Psalm 126:5,6

As we see in this passage, there is a special joy that comes only from sowing and reaping. That is why the Lord tells us He "prizes" a cheerful giver. Continual, overflowing joy is supposed to be the identifying characteristic of the one who makes a lifestyle of giving. That joy is not only a blessing, it is also a powerful weapon for spiritual warfare.

A number of years ago, the Lord gave me a message for the Body of Christ. After I began to preach it, people heard it and responded to it so well that it was recorded on cassette and video tape and published in book form. It has been the most popular and most widely appreciated message I have ever presented.

The title of that message is simple: "If Satan Can't Steal Your Joy, He Can't Keep Your Goods." The message you are reading right now is sort of a sequel to that one. I suppose this one could be entitled, "Joy II." The emphasis of this message is as simple as its title: we must have the joy of the Lord if we are to have and keep the blessings of God.

Especially in times of economic crisis, such as those we are now facing on a worldwide scale.

Nehemiah 8:10 declares: *...the joy of the Lord is your strength.* Without the strength of joy, many believers will fail in the hard times which lie ahead.

Right now twenty percent of the Body of Christ is carrying eighty percent of the load of the Church. Twenty percent of God's people are doing most of the giving, while the other eighty percent are doing very little or nothing at all. That situation must change, because when hard times descend upon us, only those who have prepared themselves will overcome.

Only they will know how to win out over adversity, how to come through hardship victoriously - by sowing in time of famine. The only survivors of Satan's attack will be those whose strength comes from and rests upon a deep, abiding joy of the Lord.

As giving becomes a lifestyle, greater peace, quietness, confidence, assurance and joy will be yours.

You Reap What You Sow

If you are not happy with your life, you have no one to blame but yourself. Your life today consists of what you sowed in the past. If you don't like your crop, dig it up and plant something else. If you don't want crab grass in your yard, you dig it up and plant Bermuda grass there. Do the same thing in your life.

You were not born to be poor, any more than the earth was created to bring forth weeds, thorns and thistles. Like the earth itself, you were created to produce a good harvest of fine fruit - for yourself and for many others. If you are not enjoying "the fruits of your labor," then check your seed. Replace your old, bad seed with new, good seed.

Remember: what you sow today is what you will reap tomorrow.

I am a close friend of Charles Capps, one of the most dynamic teachers of our time. We have been friends for a number of years now. He and I used to preach together a lot, particularly all over Arkansas where Charles lives. I have stayed in his home on several occasions.

Charles lives on a large farm out in the country, not far from Little Rock, Arkansas. He has been a farmer most of his life. Every time I would go to his home, I noticed that he had cotton growing everywhere. In fact, the narrow piece of ground where we landed our airplane lay right down the middle of a cotton patch. Whenever we landed or took off, there was cotton growing on both sides of the airstrip.

But then one time I went home with Charles and the first thing I noticed was that there was no cotton. Instead, the entire place was covered with soybeans. So I asked Charles, "What happened to the cotton?"

"I didn't plant any," was his simple answer. End of conversation. Charles is a man of few words.

One year there was cotton, the next year there wasn't. When I asked why there was no cotton, he told me all the truth I needed to know: there was no cotton because he hadn't planted cotton that year! And obviously, if you don't plant cotton seed, you don't raise cotton. Even I could figure that out.

I could have asked him where all the soybeans had come from, but I already knew what he would say: "I planted them." Sure. You want soybeans, you plant soybeans. Simple.

The same is true in your life and mine. What we plant is what we get. What we sow, that shall we also reap. That's a basic spiritual principle.

A farmer's success depends entirely upon his sowing good seed and reaping good crops. In the very same way, the harvest in our lives depends totally upon what we sow. That's why Satan fights so hard against the preaching of this message. He knows it links you to God's system of prosperity.

God has declared, in the book of Genesis, that as long as the earth remains, seedtime and harvest will not cease (Geneseis 8:22). The earth itself operates on this principle. Everything we do on this planet depends upon that one central rule. That's how the earth is populated, by seedtime and harvest. Whatever the field of endeavor - finances, agriculture, industry, medicine, education, ministry - it all works on the same fundamental principle that what is sown (invested) is what is reaped (produced).

That's how we grow spiritually: by planting seeds. We give and it is given to us. We give love, and love comes back to us. We show ourselves to be friendly, and we reap friends. We give understanding to others, and we receive understanding. We listen to others, and in turn they listen to us. We give out the knowledge we have gained, and God increases that knowledge.

That's why I say that it is foolish and wrong for a person to say that he will start giving to God as soon as the Lord has made him rich. That is like a person expecting a fireplace to give off heat before he throws in any wood for it to burn. That's going at life backwards.

We all know that to get water from a pump, we must first prime the pump. We must pour into life, if we expect to get anything out of it. At this time in your life, you may be going out sowing in tears, but God has promised that you will return joyfully bearing your sheaves with you.

If you want to prosper in mind, body and spirit, then learn to sow generously into the lives of others. Whoever you are, whatever your desired harvest, you will reap just what you sow.

Sow Good Seeds

Be not deceived; God is not mocked: for whatsoever a man soweth, that shall he also reap.

For he that soweth to his flesh shall of the flesh reap corruption; but he that soweth to the Spirit shall of the Spirit reap life everlasting.

And let us not be weary in well doing: for in due season we shall reap, if we faint not.

Galatians 6:7-9

Notice the first part of verse 7. It warns us about being deceived. It is highly important that we not allow anybody to deceive us into thinking that we can reap (receive) anything that we have not first sowed (invested in faithfully and consistently). The Phillips translation of the next part of this verse says "a man's harvest in life depends entirely on that which he sows." Verse 9 counsels us not to become weary in our sowing, because if we keep it up long enough, we will reap.

Of course all this is based on the assumption that we are sowing good seed. Our harvest will be whatever we sow; therefore we must be careful about the kind of seed we plant. If we want health, we must sow seeds of health. If we want prosperity, we must sow seeds of prosperity. If we want love, we must sow seeds of love. Good crops are the result of good seed planted in good soil.

Be Not Weary; Instead, Be Disciplined

Several years ago, I began to realize that I was not in the same physical condition I had been in when I was younger. As a young man I never had to worry about my weight because I could eat anything and everything I wanted and still not gain an ounce. But somewhere around age 34 or 35 I began to notice that I was putting on a little weight. I had already recognized that I wasn't as energetic as I used to be. I got tired quicker and had less energy. I also had to admit that I was developing a good-sized "spare tire" around the middle, and I didn't like it.

I happened to have a good friend who was a former Mr. Universe. Of course, unlike me, he was all muscle. So I made up my mind that I was going to let him put me on a regimen of diet and exercise to build me up physically. So I asked my friend to come to my house in order to get me started on a good physical fitness program.

Before he arrived I went downtown and bought myself a couple of jogging suits and some running shoes and everything I thought I would need to get in shape. Then I cleared out my garage to make room for all that new fitness equipment I was going to buy and use.

So, "Mr. Universe" arrived by plane and I went out to the airport to welcome him. Right away we set in on my new fitness program. The first day we worked out really hard - and it felt great. I could hardly wait for the next day. I had the best of intentions. I was going to get up bright and early at 5:30 every morning and start working out.

Of course, you know what happened. The next morning I was so stiff and sore, I could hardly move a muscle, much less spring out of bed "rarin' to go." It wasn't long at all before "the new had worn off" that idea. But I kept it up for three or four days. Then I went in to show off my new physique to Carolyn. I assumed my best "Mr. Universe" pose and asked her, "Well, do you see any difference?"

"In what?" she asked.

"In me," I answered. "In my physique."

"No."

Naturally that hurt my feelings, and my pride. I thought that with all that healthy eating and sweat and hard work surely I must look like Superman by that time.

A short time later I again went to the airport, this time to see my muscle-man friend off on a jet. Can you guess what I did as soon as he was on his way home? That's right, I stopped off at the nearest Mexican food place and stuffed my mouth with tacos, enchiladas and guacamole!

What happened? I got "weary in well doing." I gave up and went right back to my old undisciplined, unhealthy lifestyle.

But then later on, my conscience got to bothering me. So a few months later I went back on my diet and exercise program. This time I didn't call my friend to come get me started. I just did it on my own initiative. It lasted about a week.

Once again I got "weary in well doing" and quit. Despite my good intentions, in spite of all my cherished hopes and dreams for physical self-improvement, the plain truth is that I was just too undisciplined to stick with it long enough to see any positive results. So I gave up and quit.

It's the same with the lifestyle of giving. It's easy to make all kinds of resolutions about being a faithful, consistent giver. You can even start tithing and giving regularly.

But if you're not careful, the first thing you know, you'll start asking yourself if maybe you weren't a little foolish. You'll get to wondering if it really works.

Well, the end of that story about my weight and exercise program is this: I have since gone on a sensible program, one that I can live with and keep up. I do eat right now, and I exercise regularly and wisely. Why? What happened? I finally took authority over my own body. I learned the best and most difficult exercise in the whole world: the exercise of self-discipline!

Don't be so quick to give up. Give as the Spirit of the Lord directs you and make it your lifestyle. Be sensitive to His leading and do what He tells you. Obedience opens the door to miracles.

Finally, don't lose heart or become discouraged. Don't become "weary in well doing." Instead, be disciplined. Keep on sowing those seeds into the work of God. The Lord Himself has promised that you will reap, if you "faint not."

Keep sowing. It won't always be easy, but the results will be well worth it.

5

WHY YOUR GIVING IS IMPORTANT TO GOD

5

WHY YOUR GIVING IS IMPORTANT TO GOD

In the last two chapters we talked about the benefits of godly giving, the increased fruits of righteousness and the joy which that giving produces. We saw what our giving does: it releases our faith in God's faithfulness; it establishes God's Covenant in our lives; it links us to God and releases His power on our behalf; it enlarges our capacity to receive more from God and of God; and it increases our fruits of righteousness which include peace, quietness, confidence and assurance; and it brings us joy.

Now all that is wonderful. It is truly marvelous. And I thank and praise God for all of it. But I must point out that all of these things are primarily concerned with what our faithful, obedient, godly giving does for us. Now in this last chapter I would like to focus a bit on what our giving does for others, for the Lord Himself and for His ministry.

In the past few years, Satan has had a heyday. He has wreaked havoc in the church. He has tried to destroy the credibility of the ministry. Because of the lack of accountability in some ministries, much of the non-Christian world hates and mistrusts us.

The Lord has revealed something to me about this whole affair which He has instructed me to bring to the attention of Christians everywhere. He has shown me that a very similar situation existed in the past. He corrected that situation and then told the people what to do to restore His temple to its former righteous state.

Through this revelation, I believe the Lord has shown me His answer and solution to our current ministry crisis. It is this answer and solution which I now want to share with you as we labor together with all the saints to restore order, dignity and honor to God's holy temple, the Church of Jesus Christ.

The Purpose of Offerings

I would like to begin by talking about offerings, real offerings.

Furthermore David the king said unto all the congregation... because I have set my affection to the house of my God, I have of mine own proper good, of gold and silver, which I have given to the house of my God, over and above all that I have prepared for the holy house,

Even three thousand talents of gold, of the gold of Ophir, and seven thousand talents of refined silver, to overlay the walls of the houses withal:

The gold for things of gold, and the silver for things of silver, and for all manner of work to be made by the hands of artificers. And who then is willing to consecrate his service this day unto the Lord?

Then the chief of the fathers and princes of the tribes of Israel, and the captains of thousands and of hundreds, with the rulers of the king's work, offered willingly,

And gave for the service of the house of God of gold five thousand talents and ten thousand drams, and of silver ten thousand talents, and of brass eighteen thousand talents, and one hundred thousand talents of iron.

And they with whom precious stones were found gave them to the treasure of the house of the Lord...

Then the people rejoiced, for that they offered willingly, because with perfect heart they offered willingly to the Lord: and David the king also rejoiced with great joy.

1 Chronicles 29:1, 3-9

In this passage we read that David took up an offering which was the equivalent of 415.5 million American dollars! And over 100 million of that amount came directly from David personally.

When it came time to start collecting goods for the building of the temple of the Lord, David stood in front of the people of Israel and announced that he was going to take up an offering and that he was going to give the first 88 million dollars. Then he added another 14 million to what he had already pledged.

Afterwards he challenged the rest of the nation to join with him and they gave over 300 million dollars more. This was just from the people of God; no outsiders were involved.

What do you think would happen to the Church of Jesus Christ if God Himself were to supernaturally bless us with wealth beyond our wildest imagination? What do you think our next offering would be like? Possibly we could beat the offering received by David.

But no, the Body of Christ is satisfied with just barely making it through life, then complaining because someone else in the Body is being blessed more than they are. All that must change. Because we have got to get this Gospel out to the uttermost part of the earth. To do that, there must be a dramatic change in the financial condition of the Church of the Living God!

Paul wrote to the Philippians: *I know how to be abased...* (Phil. 4:12). Notice that he said he knew **how** to be abased, he didn't say he always was in that condition. He didn't say that it was God's will for him to be abased. We know this was not God's will for Paul because the apostle goes on in that same verse to say, *...and I know how to abound...*

When you and I learn how to use our faith while we are abased, then, like Paul, we can be trusted by God to abound.

At one time or another we have all been abased. Each one of us has had some limitation imposed upon us. Every Christian alive has had some restriction placed upon his or her life. Throughout the ages Satan has tried his best to abase, limit, and restrict the Body of Christ. But, like Paul, we have learned to keep our faith going right in the middle of those times of trial and tribulation.

Paul said that he knew how to be abased, and how to abound. This is the lesson the Church of Jesus Christ needs to learn today.

Now you and I have both been through our times of being abased. The question is: are we ready to abound? We know what it is to be poor, but have we come to the point yet that we are ready to be prospered.

In His Word, God has promised to pour out overflowing blessings upon those who know how to keep their faith in times of adversity; those who will not give up and quit at the first sign of trouble, hardship or opposition; those who are seed-minded, not need-minded.

The Motivation for Giving

And Moses spake unto all the congregation of the children of Israel, saying, This is the thing which the Lord commanded, saying,

Take ye from among you an offering unto the Lord: whosoever is of a willing heart, let him bring it, an offering of the Lord; gold, and silver, and brass,

And blue, and purple, and scarlet, and fine linen, and goats' hair,

And rams' skins dyed red, and badgers' skins, and shittim wood,

And oil for the light, and spices for anointing oil, and for the sweet incense,

And onyx stones, and stones to be set for the ephod, and for the breastplate,

And every wise hearted among you shall come, and make all that the Lord hath commanded.

Exodus 35:4-10

Notice in verse 5 that when it comes time to bring an offering to the Lord, it is "whosoever is of a willing heart" who is to make that offering. Notice also in verse 10 that it is "every wise hearted among you" who is told to yield to the Lord's command to bring offerings into His house.

And all the congregation of the children of Israel departed from the presence of Moses.

And they came, every one whose heart stirred him up, and every one whom his spirit made willing, and they brought the Lord's offering to the work of the tabernacle of the congregation, and for all his service, and for the holy garments.

Exodus 35:20,21

God spoke, the people heard, they were wise, and they were stirred up. As a result, they brought offerings. That is an important sequence of events, one which we should note and remember.

And they came, both men and women, as many as were willing hearted, and brought bracelets, and earrings, and rings, and tablets, all jewels of gold: and every man that offered offered an offering of gold unto the Lord.

Exodus 35:22

Notice that only those who were "willing hearted" brought an offering.

And all the women that were wise hearted did spin with their hands, and brought that which they had spun, both of blue, and of purple, and of scarlet, and of fine linen.

Exodus 35:25

Also note that it was those who were "wise hearted" who worked with their hands in order to have fine goods to bring as an offering to the work of the Lord.

The children of Israel brought a willing offering unto the Lord, every man and woman, whose heart made them willing to bring for all manner of work, which the Lord had commanded to be made by the hand of Moses.

Exodus 35:29

Again it is emphasized that this was a "willing offering unto the Lord," made by those "whose heart made them willing to bring."

It seems clear enough from this passage that God desires that our offerings to Him be made from a willing heart, a wise heart, a heart which desires to give freely and abundantly.

The Result of the Offering

And all the wise men, that wrought all the work of the sanctuary, came every man from his work which they made;

And they spake unto Moses, saying, The people bring much more than enough for the service of the work, which the Lord commanded to make.

And Moses gave commandment, and they caused it to be proclaimed throughout the camp, saying, Let neither man nor woman make any more work for the offering of the sanctuary. So the people were restrained from bringing.

For the stuff they had was sufficient for all the work to make it, and too much.

Exodus 36:4-7

As a direct result of the people's being stirred up to make a freewill offering to the work of the Lord, there was such an outpouring of gifts that Moses had to command the people to stop bringing. They had already brought enough, and even more than could ever be used.

When was the last time your church was so stirred up to make an offering that so much was received there was more than could possibly be used? Yet I believe this is exactly what the Lord desires to happen.

God has a work going on today, just as He did in the days of Moses and the children of Israel. Just as in those days, He is building His temple. Despite all the flaws, abuses and failures which surround us, God hasn't become discouraged. He hasn't given up and quit. His work goes on. It is even more important today than it was in Old Testament times. In Exodus He was erecting a physical temple of stone and mortar. Today He is building a living temple - the Church, the Body of Christ.

Satan has opposed the work of the Lord at every stage. He is still opposing it today, just as he did in the days of Moses and Solomon and Ezra. Read your Bible - Satan has tried to stop the work of God for thousands of years. Yet the Lord always emerges victorious, and He will continue to do so in our day, despite scandal, accusation, ridicule and unbelief.

The Need for the Offering

Satan cannot stop anything the Lord is doing. All he can do is distract God's people. In the days of Moses, there was a work going on, the building of the tabernacle. The Lord commanded the people to bring their offerings, and their hearts were stirred to respond.

I believe there needs to be a new stirring in the hearts of the individual members of the Body of Christ in this crucial hour. Each one of us needs to become willing-hearted and wise-hearted enough to give generously and sacrificially to complete the work which has already been started.

There are millions of lives to be touched and changed. There are millions of people around the globe who still need to hear the Gospel and be saved. There are many who need to receive the healing power of God. This work of the Lord must go on. We cannot sit back and let the Devil talk us out of giving just because there have been misfortunes, problems, sins and scandals in the Christian ministry.

The people of God must have their hearts stirred so they will willingly bring their offerings to the Lord for His service. In Moses' day, the people brought so much they had to be told to stop, that there was already more than could be used. I wish to God every church in America had this problem! I look forward to the day this sort of thing is a weekly occurrence.

These people weren't giving to Moses; they were giving to the work of the Lord. Your gift is not made to any certain man or woman or local church or television ministry, it is made to God Himself. If the person or group receiving your gift turns out to be dishonest, unreliable or immoral, that is not your fault, nor should it affect your giving. Just ask the Lord what to do about your gifts and where they should continue to go for the sake of building His kingdom on earth.

Preparation for the Offering

Notice verse 2 of that passage in 1 Chronicles 29. David told the people, *I have prepared with all my might for the house of my God...*

Friend, you and I have got to be prepared in the short time which is left to us. We must be prepared to plant our seed-gifts into the crucial work of the Lord.

Notice verse 3: Moreover, *...I have set my affection to the house of my God...* That is the key to godly giving: to set our affections to the house of God.

In Colossians 3:2 the Apostle Paul tells us: *Set your affection on things above, not on things on the earth.* The "things that are above" refer to the things of God - the things of the Spirit. The "things on the earth" refer to material wealth and riches, carnal desires.

If you and I will do what David did, if we will prepare with all our might for the Lord's house, and set our affections on the things of God, then our hearts will be made willing and wise. We will give freely and generously because we will want to have a part in the building of God's holy kingdom.

The Joy of Offering

Notice what happened because David and the people of Israel set their affections on the things of the Lord:

Then the people rejoiced, for that they offered willingly, because with perfect heart they offered willingly to the Lord: and David the king also rejoiced with great joy.

1 Chronicles 29:9

These people had just given the equivalent of 415.5 million dollars to the work of the Lord, and instead of being angry, worried or despondent they were rejoicing! Twice in this one verse the Bible says that they were rejoicing because they had given willingly. Obviously, to these people giving to the Lord was not a chore, a burden, a duty or an obligation, it was a "great joy!"

Well it would seem that the Body of Christ has a long way to go yet, doesn't it? Can we all honestly say that we have gotten to the place in our Christian lives that giving has truly become a "great joy?" And yet that is exactly what it is supposed to be, what it is meant to be, what it was designed by God to be. Giving, is the essence of living, the very reason for our being.

Godly giving is a joy!

God's Cleansing of His Temple

Hezekiah was twenty-five years old when he became the king of Judah, and he reigned twenty-nine years, in Jerusalem...

His reign was a good one in the Lord's opinion, just as his ancestor David's had been.

In the very first month of the first year of his reign, he reopened the doors of the Temple and repaired them.

He summoned the priests and Levites to meet him at the open space east of the Temple, and addressed them thus:

Listen to me, you Levites. Sanctify yourselves and sanctify the Temple of the Lord God of your ancestors - clean all the debris from the holy place.

For our fathers have committed a deep sin before the Lord our God; they abandoned the Lord and his Temple and turned their backs on it...

But now I want to make a covenant with the Lord God of Israel so that his fierce anger will turn away from us. My children, don't neglect your duties any longer, for the Lord has chosen you to minister to him...

They in turn summoned their fellow Levites and sanctified themselves, and began to clean up and sanctify the Temple, as the king (who was speaking for the Lord) had commanded them.

2 Chronicles 29:1-6,10,11,15 (TLB)

Notice the first thing that Hezekiah did when he became king. He saw that the work of the Lord had been suffering. He recognized that the spiritual leadership of the nation had fallen down on its job. He realized that the temple of the Lord needed to be cleansed and repaired. He understood that the priests and Levites, the spiritual leaders, needed to be purged. And he immediately set in to carry out the will of the Lord.

I submit to you that in our day the same kind of thing has been going on. The work of the Lord has suffered, the spiritual leadership has not lived up to its duty and responsibility and high calling. The temple of the Lord (the Body of Christ) is in dire need of cleansing and "repair." The leaders of God's people have become filled with filthiness and "debris" and are in need of cleansing and sanctifying.

But I also submit to you that God has already begun this work. There is a cleansing and sanctifying process taking place right now in the Church. The Lord has taken it upon Himself to bring about a cleansing by the washing of the water of the Word, that He might sanctify unto himself a holy people, that we might become a Church without spot, wrinkle or blemish.

Whether you are yet aware of it or not, there is a cleansing of the Church going on right now. There is a purging of the spiritual leadership taking place.

Notice verse 10 in which King Hezekiah says that he is making a new covenant with the Lord so He will turn away from the people His fierce anger. Then in verse 11 he says, *Children, don't neglect your duties any longer, for the Lord has chosen you to minister to him...* In other words, he is saying, "ministers, don't be negligent any longer." I believe that is the primary problem with the spiritual leadership today. They have been neglecting their duties. The problem is not really so much a lack of sincerity or vision. It is simply a lack of consistency and diligence.

Notice also what the Levites did in response to the word of the Lord which they received through Hezekiah: *They in turn summoned their fellow Levites and sanctified themselves, and began to sanctify and clean up the Temple...* (v.15) There are a lot of preachers and Christian teachers who are now getting on their knees and repenting. As they do, they are able to begin to lead the people into a thorough cleansing of the Church.

The spiritual leadership of our day is purging itself, getting rid of negligence and inconsistency, returning to the Lord and His service. Once again the Lord is cleansing His temple.

Encourage the Ministry

Hezekiah now organized the priests and Levites into service corps...

In addition, he required the people in Jerusalem to bring their tithes to the priests and Levites, so that they wouldn't need other employment but could apply themselves fully to their duties as required in the law of God.

The people responded immediately and generously with the first of their crops and grain, new wine, olive oil, money, and everything else - a tithe of all they owned, as required by law to be given to the Lord their God. Everything was laid out in great piles.

The people who had moved to Judah from the northern tribes and the people of Judah living in the provinces also brought in the tithes of their cattle and sheep, and brought a tithe of the dedicated things to give to the Lord, and piled them up in great heaps.

The first of these tithes arrived in June, and the piles continued to grow until October.

When Hezekiah and his officials came and saw these huge piles, how they blessed the Lord and praised his people!

2 Chronicles 31:2,4-8 (TLB)

Here we see that despite what had gone on in the past, the king commanded the people to once again give generously to those in the Lord's service. The people knew what had been the condition of the temple and the state of affairs among God's servants, yet they gave willingly and joyfully into the Lord's work. The result was such an overflowing abundant offering that it was piled up in heaps.

Notice the *King James Version* of verse 4:

Moreover he commanded the people that dwelt in Jerusalem to give the portion of the priests and the Levites, that they might be encouraged in the law of the Lord.

Friend, it is time for the people of God to once again give to the work of the Lord so that His ministers might be encouraged. For too long now the ministry has been under attack. People have become suspicious and distrustful and have withheld their tithes and gifts. As a result, many ministries of all kinds and all sizes have suffered tremendous financial setbacks and hardships. It is time for the people of God to encourage His ministers.

I thank God that in the midst of these troubled times my partners have not quit on me. Oh, I always need more of them and more from them. But I am thankful that the ones I do have are faithful and loyal. My little "Gideon's army" has done wonders, and I praise and thank the Lord for giving them to me. They have stuck by me and my ministry "through thick and thin." But that is what all Christians need to do in these demanding times.

The ministers have made mistakes, just as the priests and Levites did in the days of King Hezekiah. But now, it is time to encourage them, as the Israelites did in response to the word of the Lord given to them through their king. That is the same word of the Lord which I am now bringing to you through this book.

I am convinced that Satan is not going to win, because the Body of Christ is going to rally. They are going to once again give wholehearted support to the Lord's work and to His servants.

The message you have read in these pages has been a prophetic word from the Lord. It is my prayer: 1) that you will take it to heart and do your part by giving not only your tithes but also generous offerings, 2) that you will "divide your gifts among many," 3) that you will be faithful in supporting your local church, and 4) that you will go beyond all that and give to encourage home and foreign missions, radio and television ministries, and any other outreaches which the Lord lays upon your heart.

Closing Prayer

Father, in the name of the Lord Jesus Christ, I have delivered Your Word under the unction of the Holy Spirit. I have told Your people what You instructed me to tell them. I have given them the prophetic message You laid upon my heart.

I thank You, Father, that You will confirm Your Word with signs following. Let there be a stirring in the hearts of the people. Give them, I pray, a willing mind and heart. May what has been presented in these pages break through the confusion and disorder, and focus the eyes of Your people back on Jesus and on the work that You have set before us. It must be finished. It must be carried through to completion.

Lord, we agree together that there will be a change. Instead of twenty percent of the Church carrying eighty percent of the load, every member of the Body of Christ will be doing his or her part, both in the local church and in the other ministries which You have raised up. Every good work will go forth and every minister will fulfill the vision You have given.

Now, Lord, as Your people begin to give once again into Your work, use those gifts to encourage the ministry. We have been refreshed, now help us to refresh Your ministers and servants. As we plant our seed, we are expecting the fruits of righteousness to be increased in us so that we can walk forth in this world in peace, quietness, confidence and assurance. And as we give, we expect our joy to increase. We don't know how You will supply our every need, but we know You will. And we thank You for it, in Jesus' mighty name. Amen.

References

Holy Bible: New International Version (NIV). Copyright 1973, 1978, 1984 by the New York International Bible Society. Used by permission of Zondervan Bible Publishers.

The King James Version, Royal Publishers, Nashville, TN.

The Living Bible (TLB). Copyright 1971 owned by assignment by Illinois Regional Bank N.A. (as trustee). Used by permission of Tyndale House Publishers, Inc., Wheaton, IL 60189. All rights reserved.

The New Testament in Modern English, Revised Edition. Copyright 1958, 1959, 1960, 1972 by J.B. Phillips. Macmillian Publishing Company.

The Revised Standard Version of the Bible. New Testament section copyright 1946, Old Testament section copyright 1952 by Division of Christian Education of the National Council of the Churches of Christ in the United States of America.

The Holy Bible: From the Ancient Eastern Text (Lamsa), George M. Lamsa. Copyright 1933, 1957 by A.J. Holmon Co., Philadelphia, PA. Harper and Row, Publishers Inc.

Other Books By Jerry Savelle

Walking In Divine Favor
Turning Your Adversity Into Victory
Honoring Your Heritage Of Faith
Don't Let Go Of Your Dreams
Faith Building Daily Devotionals
The Force of Joy
If Satan Can't Steal Your Joy,
He Can't Keep Your Goods
A Right Mental Attitude
The Nature Of Faith
The Established Heart
Sharing Jesus Effectively
Turning Your Dreams Into Reality
How To Overcome Financial Famine
You're Somebody Special To God
Leaving The Tears Behind

**For a complete list of tapes, books and videos
by Jerry Savelle, write:**

**Jerry Savelle Ministries International
P.O. Box 748
Crowley, Texas 76036
(817) 297-3155**

Dr. Jerry Savelle is a noted author, evangelist, and teacher who travels extensively throughout the United States, Canada, and around the globe. He is president of Jerry Savelle Ministries International, a ministry of many outreaches devoted to meeting the needs of believers all over the world.

Well known for his balanced Biblical teaching, Dr. Savelle has conducted seminars, crusades, and conventions for over twenty-five years as well as ministering in thousands of churches and fellowships. He is in great demand today because of his inspiring message of victory and faith and his vivid, and often humorous, illustrations from the Bible. He teaches the uncompromised Word of God with a power and an authority that is exciting, but with a love that delivers the message directly to the spirit man.

In addition to his International Headquarters in Crowley, Texas, Dr. Savelle is also founder of JSMI - Africa, JSMI - United Kingdom, JSMI - South Africa and JSMI - Tanzania. In 1994, he established the JSMI Bible Institute and School of World Evangelism. It is a two-year school for the preparation of ministers to take the Gospel of Jesus Christ to the nations of the world.

The missions outreaches of his ministry extend to over 50 countries around the world. JSMI further ministers the Word of God through an extensive prison ministry outreach.

Dr. Savelle has authored many books and has an extensive video and cassette teaching tape ministry and a nationwide television broadcast. Thousands of books, tapes, and videos are distributed around the world each year through Jerry Savelle Ministries International.